S. Ruth Wheeler
1978

It Takes a Long Time
to Become Young

It Takes a Long Time to Become Young

AN ENTERTAINMENT IN THE FORM OF A DEC-
LARATION OF WAR ON THE MINDLESS YOUTH
CULT THAT HAS OUR TIME IN ITS GRIP: DE-
MORALIZING OUR PEOPLE, WEAKENING OUR
SYSTEM, DEPLETING OUR ENERGY, FEEDING
OUR DEPRESSION, WASTING OUR EXPERIENCE,
BETRAYING OUR DEMOCRACY, AND BLOWING
OUT BRAINS.

Garson Kanin

DOUBLEDAY & COMPANY, INC.
GARDEN CITY, NEW YORK
1978

Library of Congress Cataloging in Publication Data

Kanin, Garson, 1912–
It takes a long time to become young.

1. Retirement—United States.   I. Title.
HQ1062.K34   301.43′5
ISBN 0-385-12475-9
Library of Congress Catalog Card Number 77–89416

It Takes a Long Time
to Become Young

The muddle of old age is not that one is old, but that one is young.

Oscar Wilde

I am at home, alone. My wife is in Hollywood, making a movie. Watching the "Six O'Clock News" on television, I have the unsettling feeling that I have seen it all before. An editorial comes on. As a rule, this is a bathroom break—but tonight's subject catches me, holds me.

I hear myself talking back to the talking head which is saying:

> Retirement is punching a time clock for the last time. It's a promise, and it's a threat.
>
> Retirement promises leisure, relaxation, a time to pursue a neglected hobby, and to collect rewards for long labor: pension, Social Security, maybe a gold watch.
>
> But retirement is also a threat. For many workers, it is a time for losing, losing income, losing a sense of worth, losing friends, losing something to do. It can be, medical experts say, a killer. Being forced into retirement and out of the work force can damage

the health of an older man, according to a committee of the American Medical Association. So it's no surprise that organizations of older people these days are battling against forced retirement, which is being challenged in the courts and Congress.

A major case, in fact, should soon be decided by the Supreme Court. It involves Robert Murgia, a Massachusetts policeman who was forced to retire because he had reached the age of fifty. His lawyers argue that forced retirement based on age is unconstitutional and unwise. Workers, the lawyers argue, can be productive long past retirement age.

Well, that is certainly true. But in a practical sense, how can businesses and other institutions deal with the inevitable decline of aging workers if they cannot make them retire at some age?

The point here is that there are flaws in any retirement system based on age. But those who criticize mandatory retirement should tell us how it can be done better. Can physical tests be devised that fairly can tell older people when they should retire? We doubt it.

As a practical matter, we think mandatory retirement does make sense if the age chosen is a reasonable one.

And that's the opinion of the management of CBS News.

Now a disembodied voice:

> Those differing with CBS editorials are invited to request time to reply.

"Damn right. I will!" I yelled.

Noble resolutions of this sort usually fade by morning. This time, however, the fitful night was spent in troubled sleep, alternating with angry wakefulness, during which endless drafts of replies were composed.

In the morning, exhausted, I phoned CBS and requested time to reply.

"There've been loads of others," a young woman said. "Organizations as well as individuals. But send yours in and it'll be considered."

"All right."

"You have ninety seconds."

"*Ninety!?*"

"Yes, the same as Peter Kohler's editorial."

"That was more than ninety."

"No. And remember—you've got to state your name and affiliation—so it comes down to more like *eighty* seconds."

"Thank you very much."

At this point it all seemed a futile and fruitless gesture, but there was no turning back. I hammered away at my reply. Eighty seconds! Impossible.

Two nights later, *mine* was the talking head on the CBS News:

> I'm Garson Kanin of New York, replying as a private citizen to a recent Channel Two editorial which closed by saying, "As a practical

matter, we think mandatory retirement does make sense if the age chosen is a reasonable one."

Nonsense!

Working men and women should retire for two reasons only: if they *want* to retire or if they are unable to function. These conditions may occur at age forty-two, or twenty-six, or thirty-eight, or eighty-seven.

Setting a precise age is folly. We are all—thank God and nature—different. I know many young people in their seventies—and a few old fogies of forty.

As a man condemned to death reckons his remaining days, he is conditioned. Four more—three more—two—one—and he's ready for it.

A man who is told that on his sixty-fifth birthday he will be no longer useful, lives through the same sort of agonizing count-down—and finally allows a silly system to transform him overnight into a superfluous nonentity.

What's the difference between killing a man and not allowing him to live?

Of all the dangerous and destructive "isms" that have plagued this century, ageism is the most stupid.

It's time to declare war on the mindless Youth Cult that has our time in its grip: demoralizing our people, weakening our system, depleting our energy, feeding our depression, wasting our experience, betraying our democracy, and blowing out brains.

Then it began. Phone calls, letters, telegrams, strangers stopping me on the street. Apparently, many had talked back to a television set the night of the editorial.

The train of thought and the strain of feeling engendered that night continue.

Call it paradoxical or call it nutty, but consider these disparate facts and figures: For the past two hundred years the scientific community has worked not only diligently but successfully in an effort to extend the life span.

Two hundred years ago, when our Republic was born, the American's average life expectancy was 33 years for men, 35 for women.

By 1876 it had risen to 42 and 45, respectively.

Today, men and women can count on 70-odd, barring accident or fatal disease.

Gerontological scientists state that there are more older people alive in the world today than the total of all the older people who ever lived in the world before.

In *The Stress of Life*, Dr. Hans Selye writes:

> Among my autopsies (and I have performed quite a few) I have never seen a man who died of old age. . . . We invariably die because one vital part has worn out too early in proportion to the rest of the body. . . . True

physiologic aging is not determined by the time elapsed since birth, but by the total amount of wear and tear to which the body has been exposed. There is, indeed, a great difference between physiologic and chronologic age. One may be much more senile in body and mind, and much closer to the grave at forty than another person at sixty.

And in a recent interview, Dr. Selye said: "Every person must find his own way. Every person has a different level of stress. You can't force a turtle to run like a race horse, and you will kill a race horse if you make it slow down like a turtle. I myself am a race horse. I get up at four A.M. every day and work fourteen hours a day and bicycle around the university. I have worked fourteen hours a day since I was a student, and my mother said it would kill me. I do not need to work, financially, but if I did not work, I would die. I know a race horse named Walter—he is an actual race horse—and he is twenty years old. He runs as fast as he can even though he has nowhere to go. He needs to race."

So. We are living longer and longer, perhaps better and better. We smile, secure in our superiority over our forebears. We laugh at them as we do at old silent movies: "What dresses!" "What kisses!"

We have advanced. All honor to the men and women of medicine and science and research who have made it possible.

There is a body of medical opinion which holds that the mind is still young at 50, that the brain does not reach its full capacity until about 60. From 60 to 80, it may be that mental efficiency declines slowly, very slowly, which means that at 80 one can be as productive mentally as one was at 30, with the considerable advantage of accumulated information which, coupled with experience, becomes wisdom.

In the last few decades, geriatrics and gerontology have attracted specialists who are working, they tell us, "not merely to add years to life, but to add life to years."

Bravo. But hold. Here is the paradox—or the nuttiness: In *other* parts of our society, powers with business or industrial or financial or political or mysterious concerns are pulling in the opposite direction.

Yes, men and women are being enabled to grow older and older, but at the same time are being declared obsolete earlier and earlier.

Time was when men retired from businesses or occupations or professions or academic activities in their seventies—if they wished to do so. By that time most of them had had enough of whatever it was they had been doing for so many long years.

Then the Big Brothers began to take over, along with the actuaries and the efficiency experts and the data-computer boys. Human beings became units; classifiable (to them) entities.

Companies and corporations and institutions were persuaded that it was to their economic and operational advantage to dispose of employees who had reached the age of, say, 68. This number soon fell to 65, to 64, all at once to 62, until now many organizations use 60 as the cut-off point. What next? Fifty, as in the case of Robert Murgia? Forty-four? Forty?

How did it all begin, anyway?

In the hearty reorganization of life following World War II, the statistical sciences came to the fore. Data computers took their place beside jet-powered planes.

To understand the speed and vigor with which these new elements developed, consider that more than half the jobs now being performed by working Americans did not even *exist* at the end of World War II.

The population had exploded and become fair game for commercial exploitation. What can we sell them? And how much of it? And for how much? Most important—who are "them"?

Ask the computers, the new know-everythings. The computers smugly replied that the bulk of our population lay on the younger side. A piddling 8 per cent was over 65 and so hardly mattered. A massive proliferation of teenagers. Get a fix on them. Plenty of twenties-to-thirties. After that, the age groups showed a diminishing descent.

"Concentrate on the young!" ordered the omnipotent thinking machine. And Big Business, ever eager to have its decisions made for it mechanically, thus avoiding the daring of instinct and the labor of investigation, complied at once.

Youth was served—with what it wanted, was *told* it wanted and needed and could not do without.

"Don't trust anyone over thirty!" What ever happened to that asinine, divisive, and useless dictum so popular in the sixties? Answer: It has been abashedly abandoned because its perpetrators are now *themselves* over 30.

The evils of ageism concern the young as well as the old. If they live, they will grow older. Some will succeed, others fail. In their number will be found illness and health, wealth and poverty, happiness and misery, fulfillment and frustration—but they know that they will all grow older, and older still—reaching, in time, the critical stage now occupied by their beset elders.

When Youth became Big Business, the economy pursued it, wooed it, seduced it. Automobiles, clothing, cosmetics, books, music, television, movies, household appliances, homes, holidays, gadgetry—all were aimed at the so-called Young, and often the Young responded as programmed.

The fact that many of the Old were paying the bills was not regarded as significant. Young was "in." Old was "out." Older men began to touch up their hair, to buy hairpieces, to lie about their ages. For women, hot pants came into vogue. Short skirts, shorter still—up, up—was there to be no limit? (Some of us hoped not.)

Speed. Faster cars. Higher speed limits. Swifter travel. The Jet Set was born.

Speed reading. Graduates of these courses prided themselves on being able to read in less than an hour the novel that had taken the author four years to write.

Fast food. Ray Kroc, an energetic hamburger salesman from Chicago, bought an obscure California business called McDonald's and developed it into the most successful food operation the world has ever known. *More than 26 billion sold.* Is it possible to conceive of 26 billion sandwiches? No army can withstand the strength of a hamburger whose time has come.

The mania for speed made for the easy marketability of instant ecstasy by way of pot, LSD, and glue sniffing. Instant poverty through filthy jeans and bare feet in the city streets came into vogue. Better roads to euphoria were shunted aside, labeled "square." It takes effort and concentration and, above all, time to marshal one's sense and senses.

Part of this avidity to live in a hurry is surely occasioned by the prevalent belief that life these days has been made virtually intolerable for the elderly. So live *now*, kids! Later it's hell.

Is it too late to reshape our thinking and feeling and practice in this life-and-death matter?

Some progress may be made by legislation, but there never was a law without a loophole.

What is needed is the establishment of a fashion—everyone wants to be in fashion—that will develop into a tradition.

As the generations cross lines to mix and mingle, as they tear down artificial barriers and begin to communicate honestly, they will find that they are more alike than they are different, that they have a great deal to gain from this much-needed and viscerally desired social intercourse. Fashion and facts can lead the way.

No wise man ever wished to be younger.
                                    Jonathan Swift

Who is this Robert Murgia mentioned in the CBS editorial and why has his case—which "should soon be decided by the Supreme Court"—become a *cause célèbre?*

Robert D. Murgia was born in Andover, Massachusetts, on July 23, 1922.

His Uncle Harold was a State Trooper, and young Bobby idolized him. Any boy loves to boast, "My uncle's a cop," but imagine the added glamour and schoolyard status Bobby achieved with "My uncle's a State Trooper!"

Who knows what road his life might have taken, what aspiration he might have dared, had it not been for this happenstance? But from the first, Bob Murgia's ambition was clear. He wanted to become a State Trooper. He recalls how, on visits to Uncle Harold's house, he would sneak up to the bedroom, lock the door, and try on Uncle Harold's uniforms. No matter that they were twice his size. He would fill them on some great day in the future. He saw to it that his education in the Massachusetts public schools was directed to that end. Following high school and college, there was Army service, after which he studied, prepared, competed. On April 7, 1948, he was appointed to the Uniformed Branch of the Massachusetts State Police.

He served with distinction in every rank and office he held, was several times cited for bravery and for action beyond the call of duty; and performed a number of heroic acts that were reported on the front page of the Boston newspapers.

During his twenty-four years in the State Police, Robert Murgia lost only four days because of illness—an average of one every six years. On March 1, 1967, he was appointed Lieutenant Colonel, the highest rank in the Uniformed Branch of the Massachusetts State Police.

In March 1972, he was given his routine, mandatory physical examination by the State Police Surgeon and declared to be fully qualified to continue his duties.

Then, in his morning mail on May 9, 1972, he received a bombshell letter from the Massachusetts Board of Retirement:

> According to the birth record on file with this Board, you will attain age 50 on 7–23–72, the maximum age for Group 3 in which you are classified.
>
> In accordance with Section 5(1)(a) of chapter 32 of the General Laws, you must retire for superannuation as of the date on which your 50th birthday occurs.

This vigorous, athletic, entirely competent and experienced officer is informed that he is superannuated—which means, according to Webster's New International Dictionary, "Out-of-date or stale; disqualified or rejected on account of antiquity."

Murgia was clearly not stale. He *was* being disqualified and rejected, but could not find it within himself to accept the idea that he was either out-of-date or antique.

He decided to *refuse* to retire voluntarily, and on July 7, 1972, entered a civil action in the United States District Court, charging that the mandatory retirement statute denied him equal protection under the law.

The State argued that it had no alternative under the Massachusetts General Laws.

The District Judge dismissed Murgia's complaint because, he ruled, there was a failure to raise a substantial constitutional question. Murgia's attorneys appealed to the United States Court of Appeals, which on September 10, 1973, *reversed* the judgment of the District Court.

The legal battle in which Robert Murgia was involved was complexly joined. Finally a three-judge court took the matter under advisement.

The depositions of three physicians were put into evidence. The distinguished Dr. Thomas Royle Dawber testified that the aging process differs vastly from one individual to another and that medical testing provides reasonably accurate predictions of fitness. Dr. Thomas Silva, Jr., physician for the Boston Celtics, testified that men over 50 were perfectly capable of performing the physical duties that might be required of a State Police officer. Col. Paul Murphy,

15

the State Police Surgeon, testified that he had personally examined Colonel Murgia and found him fully capable of performing the duties of a State Police officer.

Murgia's attorneys argued that an individual's ability to continue in his employment after the age of 50 and prior to the conventional retirement age of 65 was a matter that could be determined only on an individual basis.

Note that even Murgia's hired advocates fell into the trap of referring to "the conventional retirement age of sixty-five" and appeared to be willing to accept without challenge his retirement had the specified age been 65.

They further reported that detectives in the State Police, called upon to perform similar functions as the Uniformed Branch, were permitted to continue their employment until the age of 65, and that police officers in the cities and towns of the Commonwealth of Massachusetts were also permitted to continue to age 65.

And was not sex discrimination involved, since women in the State Police were permitted to continue their employment beyond the age of 50?

On May 31, 1974, the District Court, in an opinion written by Senior Circuit Judge Bailey Aldrich, ruled in favor of Robert D. Murgia.

The Commonwealth of Massachusetts made preparations to appeal before the Supreme Court of the United States.

The matter was left unresolved while both parties prepared to wait yet another year or more for a final decision.

Everyone is too old for something, but no one is too old for everything.

Anon.

We are an ever-increasingly sports-oriented people. Can this be one of the reasons why it has been possible to foist the farce of Youth-Is-Everything upon a gullible public?

Nothing appears to be more important in our society than sports, on both the spectator and participatory levels. It is impossible to compute the number of man-hours and woman-hours devoted to them.

Is it not true that most American men turn first to the sports pages as they begin their day? Many sports vie for attention, as well as for media time and space. Their seasons overlap continually and confusingly, leaving no time unfocused on who's winning, who's losing, what's the score, and what are the odds?

A people besotted by sports is likely to have a cock-eyed view of age. A baseball player of 28 is considered elderly, a basketball player of 30 is almost unheard of, a football player of 34, a phenomenon.

In professional sports, 30 appears to be the "over-the-hill" signal. To be sure, a few freaks continue to play efficiently, even spectacularly, into their thirties. These are the exceptions, who are regarded patronizingly as oddballs—old men of 34 who still want to play. Yet consider: A baseball player aged 34 is "over the hill" professionally, but still not old enough to run for President.

In the last national election, Ronald Reagan, 64, *began* his campaign. Had he been elected, he would have been 65 when inaugurated, facing four, perhaps eight, years of service in the most demanding job on earth.

And on that very day, thousands of American men and women were unwillingly "terminated," sent home from their posts or positions for the last time, forced to adjust to a new kind of nothing life, to face families and friends—somehow humiliated, turned into superfluities for whom life apparently has no further use.

Sports are specialized disciplines that have little to do with the world's work, or with the realistic stream of life.

Adopting sports standards of age as a criterion for usefulness is utterly goofy. Moreover, marvelous feats have been performed by mature, experienced athletes.

Ballet dancers, too, are meant to fade early on and they do, except for the superior ones who refuse to follow the rule book.

On her last appearance in New York Margot Fonteyn elicited the following from a critic: "As Fonteyn has gotten older, she somehow resiliently grasped at her artistry and hung onto the core of her beauty. She offers now, and for all I know, forever, one of the most emotional experiences in dance. She throws herself at the audience with a generous grin, a feline grace, and a womanly sense of authority, wit and charm that just cannot be equaled. She is different now—no longer in her prime, but full of the autumnal glories of maturity that need no apologies."

George Balanchine recently premiered a new hour-long composition, *Vienna Waltzes,* which was acclaimed as one of his most brilliant and creative inventions. Those in his troupe say he is still probably the best dancer in the company. He is only 73.

When Martha Graham appeared as the narrator in her ballet *Lucifer,* starring Rudolf Nureyev, a reviewer wrote: "Miss Graham, at 83, looks more glamorous than ever in her rose-red caftan (by Halston), her face astonishingly youthful, her comments sharply original and wise. She is her own best saleswoman for her body philosphy."

Not long ago, Joan Sutherland, 50, appeared at the Metropolitan Opera. It was said: "Her voice sounds stronger and more lush than ever. Her coloratura ability continues to be an eighth wonder. She is aging, yes, but aging like fine wine. Such a vintage will probably never occur again in our lifetimes."

Proof positive of the idiocy of forced retirement can be had by observing how few *self-employed* people retire at age 60 or 62 or 65.

Why 65? Why not 63? Or 67?

The number was chosen by Chancellor Otto von Bismarck in 1881 when he established the first known social security program. Historians observe that he was not as interested in the welfare of German workers as he was in weakening the magnetism of socialism.

"Whoever has a pension for his old age," he said, "is more content and easier to manage than one who has no such prospect."

He chose 65 after his actuaries concluded that few Germans in the late nineteenth century lived much beyond the age of 65.

If Bismarck's information was correct almost one hundred years ago, then the corresponding figure today should be about 105.

But as other European countries followed Germany's example—although not always for the same reason—65 became the "official" number, untested, unchallenged, unquestioned.

Not until the early 1930's did the United States institute its social security system. The reformers who thought some sort of insurance necessary found themselves on the same side as the antihumanists who thought unemployment could be relieved by taking the elderly out of the work force. Together, these two pressure groups achieved the Social Security Act.

Since that time, it has grown and changed and been supplemented by plans such as Medicare, Medicaid, unemployment insurance, and various corporate or private pension plans.

Bismarck was wrong. A pension does *not* necessarily make a retiree content. The average pension in Germany today is 56 per cent of a typical worker's salary, providing he has worked for fifty years. In France, it is 40 per cent. In Japan, 35 per cent. In England, 45 per cent for married people and 29 per cent for singles. In the United States, Social Security benefits plus pensions add up to about 40 per cent of preretirement income for most workers.

Artists and writers, who are not in a position to be turned off or told to quit at a given age, generally continue to create until the end of their days; Somerset Maugham, until 92. P. G. Wodehouse published one of his most sparkling comic novels a few weeks before his death at 93. Vladimir Nabokov was still writing at peak form in his late seventies.

Carl Sandburg, Robert Frost, Archibald MacLeish, all continued to produce poetry, that most ineffable of the arts, well into their eighties.

The smash hit of London's theatrical season of late 1975 was the hilarious sex farce, *The Bed Before Yesterday*. It was written by Ben Travers, 89.

Frank Lloyd Wright's final work was even more imaginative and innovative than his earlier concepts.

In painting: Matisse, Picasso, Cassatt, Braque, Rouault, John, Benton, Pissarro, Sickert, Gainsborough, Michelangelo, Da Vinci, all give the lie to the myth that creativity fades with the passing years.

At 90, Chagall continues to work unceasingly. "I work as long as I have the strength," he says. "Without my work, my life would be idiotic. Even when I'm not working," he says, tapping his temple, "I'm working."

His new interest is The Marc Chagall Biblical Message National Museum in Nice, a nondenominational center filled with his work.

In May 1977, a series of stained-glass windows for

The Chicago Art Institute, which he had done in collaboration with Charles Marq, was installed. Each window has a theme—dance, architecture, theatre, music, poetry, and painting. "I want to tell about *all* the arts," says Chagall. And his collaborator says of him, "He has endless energy and is always enthusiastic, like a child."

When Chagall arrived at the museum in Nice on one of his periodic visits, he found a group of school-children studying its contents. He asked them if they understood his work.

"Yes! Yes!" they shouted in unison.

"That's curious," he said. "*I* do *not* understand Chagall. Not yet."

At the celebration of his seventieth birthday, Maurice Chevalier was asked, "How does it feel to be seventy?"

"Well, considering the alternative," said Maurice, "it feels wonderful."

The continuing productivity among many figures in the arts is legendary: Goethe near the end of his long life crowning his extraordinary oeuvre with *Faust*. In philosophy, science, and scholarship, further examples abound: Sigmund Freud, Albert Einstein, Albert Schweitzer, Thomas A. Edison.

Armand Hammer retired from business as he neared 80 and moved to California. Bored, he began to deal in oil to pass the time, and built one of the largest corporations in the United States, Occidental Petroleum Corporation.

And consider Grandma Moses, beginning her career in art at 72 and leaving her delicate footprints firmly in the sands of time.

Alfred North Whitehead. After a brilliant academic career at Cambridge University and the University of London, this productive mathematician, inspiring teacher, and original philosopher was forced to retire. But a mind of his sort is not easily put to rest, and Whitehead immediately looked about for something to do. When Harvard invited him to *its* Cambridge as a guest lecturer, he accepted—and stayed on for more than twenty years. It is generally agreed that however important his work was prior to his Harvard period, what he did there in his final years surpassed it. He reached more people, and had a greater influence on the forward thrust of the social order than ever before.

There are not many Whiteheads, but even some who lack direction are often propelled by circumstances onto the right road. John B. Espy is such a one.

After an outstanding career as an Air Force officer in World War II, he continued his earlier scientific education and soon found himself in the new world of data computers and thinking machines. While working for a small, successful company, he was approached by one of the massive three-letter corporations and offered a tempting salary with appealing fringe benefits. He accepted. His work with the giant firm was eminently successful and he made his way up the corporate ladder. He continued to study while working long hours and made significant contributions to his division of the company. All went swimmingly until the day of his sixty-second birthday, on which he was dismissed.

At first he was relieved to be rid at last of the pressures and responsibilities his post had put upon him. He took his wife on a 148-day cruise around the world. He had no economic problems. His pension and benefits were generous. He had made judicious investments. He was in a position to live out a comfortable life of leisure.

Upon his return home, however, he fell ill. He consulted a physician, who hospitalized him for a complete examination and exploration. Let the doctor tell the rest of the story:

"I tell you, it was *the* most baffling thing I've ever had to handle. Here was this fine, powerful specimen of a man—I knew damn near every inch of him, inside and out. I'd been his doctor, after all, for twenty-eight years—but I couldn't figure out what was wrong with him and there sure was something wrong with him. He was losing weight, his metabolism had gone haywire, his blood pressure was something out of the funny papers—jumping from low to high to down again. Mind you, this was a guy who hadn't smoked in years; alcohol consumption, a glass of wine with dinner; exercised regularly—and even *more* now that he was retired—but there was no question he was a sick man and getting sicker. His libido quit. His wife came in to see me confidentially one morning. Asked if I could recommend a sex therapist. I told her *she* was the only sex therapist I'd recommend, and we had a foolish little scrap. Then the insomnia hit him. Now, I'm not too sympathetic to insomniacs. They're usually people looking for a pill or else just lazy mollusks. I sometimes tell them, 'Well, if you can't sleep, don't go to bed. Just stay up for a few consecutive days and nights and see what happens.'

"And there was one playboy said to me, 'I've tried everything, Doc, and it's no use.'

"I said to him, 'Have you ever tried a day's work?'

"Well, thinking about this crack, and about John, I began to wonder if there was maybe some relationship between his retirement and his crack-up. We talked it over. He didn't think so. So he went on trips, played more golf, tried different diets, and got sicker and sicker. I even got him some head help, but that was no good, only confused him. Well, about this time, a buddy of his he'd worked with was also given the ol' heave-ho at sixty-two—but this other guy wasn't as phlegmatic about it as John was. This other guy was sore as a boil. He came to John and made him a proposition, which was that they should set up a little business of their own. John was this way and that way about it. After being connected for years with one of the biggest corporations in the world, being part of a tiny business seemed kid stuff, embarrassing. But when he mentioned it to me, I said, 'Well, why not give it a try? What've you got to lose? Maybe it'll make you feel better. God knows nothing *else* seems to.'

"Luckily, his buddy was one of those hotshots who

wouldn't take no and finally convinced John to go in with him. So he did.

"Right at the beginning, they didn't do all that well, that is, from a *business* standpoint. But it didn't matter because from a point of view of health and well-being, the change was more than dramatic. It was spectacular. John wasn't too aware of it, he was so concentrated and occupied, but his wife and I couldn't get over it. His nine-to-five got to be eight-to-six, then seven-to-eight, and in four months' time, he was not only as well as he'd ever been, but better. And somewhere along the line his wife came in to tell me everything had been straightened out in *that* department, too. In fact, she said it was Honeymoon Lane all over again. But that's not the end of it. Now comes a kind of O. Henry twist. A few weeks ago, John gets a call from his old company. There's a big, special hush-hush project they want to move, and for security reasons they want to have it done on the outside. So John and his partner take it on. When I had lunch with him the other day, he could hardly eat, he was laughing so hard. It turns out they're now paying him just over double what they used to pay him when he worked for *them.*"

Dr. Paul Dudley White, perhaps the outstanding cardiologist of his time, was violently opposed to men and women considering themselves old at 50 or retiring at 60 or even 70.

"This sort of thing is no longer consistent with the truth," he said. "To be sure, in the soft life of today, many individuals *are* old at fifty and most retire at sixty, but this should not and almost certainly need not be the case if adequate changes were made in the American way of life."

"To rest is to rust." So says Dr. Paul Bragg, a practicing nutritionist, unrusted at 96.

At 16, that is to say in 1897, he contracted tuberculosis. The prognosis was negative. There was apparently nothing for him to do except await adolescent death with resignation.

In desperation, his parents took him to Switzerland, where they placed him in the care of Dr. Auguste Rollier, reputed to have had a certain amount of success in treating what was then known as "consumption."

In two years, Bragg had recovered, and inspired by the example of Dr. Rollier, became one of his disciples.

In 1908 and 1912, he was a member of the United States Olympic wrestling team. In 1914, he opened the first health food store in the United States.

Dr. Bragg says he has not been to a doctor in seventy-five years.

His regime is based upon mild exercise, organic foods, and goat's milk.

His patients across the years have included Bernarr Macfadden; Mahatma Gandhi; J. C. Penney ("He died when he was only ninety-five. Ridiculous!"); Gloria Swanson; Clint Eastwood; Conrad Hilton, 90, who says, "I wouldn't be alive without him"; Jack LaLanne ("He changed and saved my life"); Muhammad Ali; and Theodore Roosevelt.

If it is true that old age is a good advertisement, Dr. Paul Bragg is one of the best for himself, for his theories, and for the glory of human possibility.

He reckons his own life expectancy at 120 and then some.

At 65, I am in far better shape than I was at 25.

I remember that troublesome 25-year-old, not as myself, but as a distant relative I would just as soon avoid.

At that age I was a mass of bad habits. I smoked foolishly, drank to excess, slept little, and popped Benzedrine tablets to keep myself awake. Headaches and bellyaches were daily companions. I was frequently involved in fist-fights and accidents. I worked carelessly and sporadically without organization or design. I was opinionated, angry, combative, competitive, envious. In short, a mess. And although now, forty years later, I have eradicated few faults, I have made considerable progress, and I trust that the next forty years will see even more.

Looking back on all this, I suppose that what has taken place principally is a shift in emphasis from the instinctive physical drives to the mental ones.

When I was young, my body controlled my mind in a runaway fashion. It has taken forty years of experience—sometimes painful, often dismaying—to put my mind in charge of the rest of me.

Long talks with many of my contemporaries and with some older friends have confirmed that this experience is not unique.

Thornton Wilder's Caesar: "To deny that one is an animal is to reduce oneself to half a man."

It is not easy to learn about "the tyranny of what *feels* good." Certainly, smoking grass provides a set of pleasurable sensations, supplying instant confidence and hope, an illusion of well-being and power. It *feels* good. Slouching in a soft armchair, beer in hand, watching a baseball game for two hours is pleasant. It *feels* good. Driving a convertible with the top down up the Pacific Coast Highway at four in the morning, at ninety miles an hour with carousing companions is exciting, and *feels* good.

But there are other things that feel good, too. The discipline of work, the joy of creating, the cherry-on-the-top of achievement, the recognition and appreciation of talent in others, the inspiration that is available in study of the greats, and the ecstasy of learning, always learning, continually learning.

It is all this that leads in time to that rarest of all attributes: applied common sense.

A few days after his inauguration as President of the United States in 1933, Franklin Roosevelt paid a call on Justice Oliver Wendell Holmes, Jr., 92. He found the Justice sitting in his library, reading Plato.

Following a few pleasantries, the President said, "May I ask why you're reading Plato, Mr. Justice?"

"Certainly, Mr. President. To improve my mind."

The National Safety Council tells us that the highest automobile accident rate involves teenage drivers. If they are lucky enough to survive, they learn to be more prudent at the wheel and, in time, leave speed and recklessness to the generations coming up behind them.

We ought to accept the fact that each decade of one's life, indeed each year, has its own colors and qualities, its strengths and weaknesses.

The species has reproduced itself billions and billions of times, yet there have never been two human beings exactly alike. We grow at varying speeds, reaching various heights. We are fat, thin, too thin, too fat, astigmatic, bald, mechanically inclined or all thumbs, coordinated or clumsy, quick to learn or slow; in short, we are individuals.

We age differently, the process being controlled by several factors: genes, heredity, environment, nutrition, climate, occupation, temperament.

An old joke: A newspaper in Miami Beach was doing a Sunday feature on the elderly inhabitants of the city. A group of reporters went about, interviewing. On a bench near the beach, one of the reporters came upon an emaciated little old man sitting quietly, looking out to sea. The reporter approached him, identified himself, and asked if he would be willing to respond to a few questions.

"Shoot," said the little old man.

"Well, first of all, do you use alcohol?"

"I don't use it," responded the little old man, "I drink it!" He cackled and blinked his eyes.

"What about smoking?"

"I've cut down on that. Doctor's orders. I don't smoke more than four packs a day now."

"Four?!"

"And six cigars."

"What about women?"

"Cut down on those, too," said the little old man. "I don't go but two or three times a day these days."

"Good God!" exclaimed the reporter. "How old are you?"

"Thirty-two," said the little old man.

Dr. Gustav Eckstein of the University of Cincinnati asserts that, from a physical and mechanical standpoint, the human body, properly treated and nourished, should last for at least 120 years. The reason so few attain that age is that we systematically *mistreat* our physical equipment. But most important, Dr. Eckstein insists, is the power of the mind, the formulation of attitudes, the quality of outlook. When these are positive, affirmative youth is automatically extended.

One of the stars of the 1975 Senior Olympics held at Irvine, California, was Mrs. Eula Weaver, who won two gold medals: one for the half-mile run, another for the mile. She was 85.

What made her triumph especially impressive was the fact that in 1972, Mrs. Weaver had been a little off her feed. She suffered from congestive heart failure, high blood pressure, angina, and arthritis.

This remarkable great-great-grandmother, instead of resigning herself to what many consider the to-be-expected ravages of old age, undertook a regenerative course of action. It involved a careful plan of diet and exercise, which steadily and gradually brought her to a point not only equal to her earlier capabilities, but surpassing them.

Eula Weaver is living proof that the aging process is reversible.

In 1974, Charlie Smith retired and moved into the Bartow, Florida, Convalescent Center. Charlie was 133 years old. He had been a slave in the mid-nineteenth century, had lived two-thirds of the history of the United States of America, and under twenty-nine of the thirty-eight Presidents.

Dr. Eckstein's idea, then, is not a fantasy. What Charlie has done, other Charlies can do.

*When I was young I used to have successes
with women because I was young. Now I
have successes with women because I am
old. Middle age was the hard part.*
                              Artur Rubinstein

"Genius," said Goethe, "is ever-renewed puberty."

Few of us aspire to so lofty an ideal as genius, but why not take a shot at ever-renewed puberty?

William James urged us to "cultivate the cheerful attitude."

We must guard against accepting myths as facts, no matter how hard the sell or how devious the reason.

Any honest man will affirm that his sexual life was least satisfying in early youth; most satisfying and effective in later life.

Yet the Youth Cult has invaded even this most intimate area of our thinking and feeling, spreading an unhealthy guilt among older people with regard to their sexual activities. Gullible men are frequently influenced by this pervasive nonsense to the point where they suffer a self-induced loss of libido and a slow going-out of one of life's most vital flames.

The same is true for women.

The mythmakers present young girls as the most coveted, desirable, and choice. The younger the better. Yet all experienced men know that these are precisely the ones who make the poorest partners.

There is a world of difference between the airy chat in the locker room and the realities of the *lit d'amour*.

When it was revealed that Representative Wayne Hays of Ohio had a mistress, one of the principal objections had to do with the idea that that was unseemly behavior for a man of 65. And when the Speaker of the House, Carl Albert, discussed the question, he ruled himself out as a subject of impropriety, saying, "Me? I'm sixty-eight years old."

Such are the powers of the overriding shibboleths by which we live, and by which our actions can be controlled.

The scientific community deals with facts rather than fantasy. Dr. Ruth B. Weg is an Associate Professor of Biology at the University of Southern California. The subject of age is her specialty. Dr. Weg identifies as misconceptions:

Sex is inappropriate for older people; interest in sex is shameful.

They are unable to perform as they get older.

They are frail; sex might even be dangerous.

"We seem to accord an older person a neuterdom, a nothingness," says Dr. Weg. "If you are over forty or fifty, or sixty-five, depending on who's talking, you're not supposed to be interested in that sort of thing."

But studies by experts in the field, such as Masters and Johnson, reveal that an interest in and capacity for sex continue into the eighties and nineties and beyond. The scientists go on to say that in later years, it may be even more important than in youth because of its effect on the morale of older people, whose self-images are constantly being battered.

Dr. Weg has dealt with the subject of impotence in men and finds that it is frequently without any physical basis.

"The expression of sexuality relates very much to other parts of our being," she says. "One reason why older men may not be able to function as well when they're over sixty-five is that some of the identity that goes with being a worker is now damaged. He feels less of a man, and he ties that into an expression that is sexual."

Discussing the question from a purely clinical and physiological standpoint, she speaks of age's advantage: "The principal change in sexuality does include a slower response. It may take a man longer to reach an erection, but it can be maintained longer.

"There's a complementary factor for women because they, too, take longer to reach a level of excitement. But women, too, have an advantage because they continue to be multiorgasmic until the day they die. And the clitoris, the primary sensate focus for women, doesn't change with age; other organs in the female genital system do."

How can we accelerate the flow of accurate scientific information to wash away the foolish cobwebs of ignorance that have entrapped so many of us for so long a time?

From thirty-five to forty-five women are old; but at forty-five the devil takes over and they become beautiful, splendid, maternal, proud. The acidities are gone and in their place reigns calm. These women are worth going out to find and because of them some men never grow old. When I see them my mouth waters.

Jean-Baptiste Troisgros

The permanent population of Martha's Vineyard used to be about six thousand, swelling to over forty thousand in the summer season.

In the past few years, there has been a dramatic increase in the number of year-round residents. These new arrivals consist mainly of retired men and women. The prevailing fashion is to winterize one's summer home, transforming it into an all-year residence. At present, 25 per cent of the island's population is made up of retirees.

As a permanent resident (nonretired) myself, I have had an opportunity to observe my good neighbors. Most of them appear to be healthy, vital, and alert people; but removed from their natural habitats and normal occupations they begin to deteriorate. It is not enough for a former university professor to putter about his house and garden seven days a week; debilitating for an experienced nurse to be consigned to a life of needlepoint and bridge.

A human being, like a muscle, can atrophy. We all know that an unused limb degenerates. The same is true of an unused skill or talent.

Many of my friends have retired voluntarily. Some are wealthy, yet the effect is the same—that of a slow, slow fading away.

Men are civilized to the extent that they are able to marshal and conquer the laws of nature rather than allow those laws to buffet them about. By the same token, it behooves us to struggle against disease and poverty and, above all, injustice.

The worst thing about life is death. That is why we all try to stave it off as long as possible. The first law of nature, we are taught, is that of self-preservation; but if you live in a society determined to eradicate you at a whimsical given point, how can you observe that law?

Senator Sam Ervin, who headed the United States Senate Watergate Committee, opposes *any* mandatory retirement age, saying, "That's about as ridiculous as saying that every bald-headed man has to retire at a certain time."

One of bureaucracy's cruelest frauds is the cynical and hypocritical kick-under-the-carpet of problems by establishing special committees, subcommittees, research groups, and task forces—then publicizing them highly. The public at large is led to believe that the formation of a committee equals the solution of the problem.

Not so.

The United States Senate has had a Special Committee on Aging since March 1961. The House of Representatives has none, although many attempts have been made to establish one.

Then there is, or was, something called "The President's Task Force on the Aging." How hopeful, how progressive the sound of that title!

In terms of achievement or accomplishment or a change in the arrangements, however, the results thus far have been nil.

The Task Force did issue a lengthy report, which concluded:

> We therefore recommend that the President establish an Office on Aging within the Executive Office of the President. We recommend that the President seek statutory authority for this office through an amendment to the Older Americans Act but that until such authority can be obtained, the President create the office by issuing an Executive Order.

Think of it. The President's Task Force on the Aging works, meets, confers, conducts research, labors, and finally brings forth a mouse in the form of a recommendation that the President establish an Office on Aging.

A simpler solution is to refuse to accept retirement. If you cannot find employment, invent it. If necessary, develop a second craft or skill, and pursue that. People turn hobbies into lucrative occupations. What is required is imagination, audacity, assertiveness, a decision to live, and the understanding that life is, as Justice Holmes reminded us, "action and passion."

Tabitha M. Powledge, of the Institute of Society, Ethics, and the Life Sciences, states: "There is evidence that work contributes positively to well-being. A study of retired university faculty members showed that although they were in good health at the time of formal retirement, those who worked afterwards at such tasks as consulting were more likely than the nonworkers to describe themselves as being in good health after retirement."

Gen. Lucius Clay, the distinguished World War II hero, was retired from the Army when he reached its mandatory retirement age. Despite the Army's view of his nonusefulness, he was not ready for oblivion. He became a Vice President of the Continental Can Corporation and served efficiently there until he reached *that* company's retirement age, whereupon he took a position with The Morgan Guaranty Trust Company, who reluctantly released him when he reached the retirement age *their* rules demanded; but General Clay went on to company after company, and at this writing, is still active and in excellent health.

The full mobilization of a nation's labor force is essential to its power and well-being. Our own labor force is plagued by three principal elements: the "drop-outs" (those who do not wish to work or who find Welfare more rewarding); the "kept-outs" (those who are discriminated against by reason of race or age or sex); and the "pushed-outs" (those who are, against their will, forced to give up their employment).

It is time to consider the adverse effects upon those surrounding the retiree: husband or wife, sons or daughters, friends or neighbors.

Inactivity breeds lassitude, boredom, frustration, anxiety, and, in time, testiness and bad temper. The partner of the victim of forced retirement must deal with problems as difficult as those which have been thrust upon the principal.

Shortly after Casey Stengel retired from his position as manager of the New York Yankees, his wife complained, "I married Casey for better or for worse, but *not* for lunch."

The solution lies in preparation. Programs for post-retirement must be planned in advance. In fact, the very act of planning provides excitement and vitality to a period of time that would otherwise be a depressing downhill journey. Such planning generates the power and strength that always accompany the acceptance of challenge.

Nothing is more stimulating than beating the odds, changing a bad system, or reversing injustice.

As more and more women enter the work force, as long-delayed equal rights become a reality, women will be dealing increasingly with job cut-off. Their problems will be compounded by the fact that, statistically, women outlive men.

Margaret Mead says of unwilling retirees: "One day they have life, the next day nothing. One reason women live longer than men is that they can continue to do someting they are used to doing, whereas men are abruptly cut off—whether they are admirals or shopkeepers."

At the turn of the century, about one-third of America's workers retired at age 65. Today, two-thirds do so. The reason for this dramatic increase is the growing custom of *forced* retirement.

The Bureau of Labor Statistics has revealed two alarming figures. One: that the life expectancy of the average male after retirement is no more than thirty to forty months. Two: that one-third of all marriages are shattered following retirement.

The suicide rate for retired men is twelve times that of those who are employed. For many of them, there is no alternative. They have been told by society, by the government, by law, that they are finished, which is why many of them decide to make it official.

Justice Felix Frankfurter's cable to Thornton Wilder on the occasion of Wilder's sixtieth birthday:

> DEAR THORNTON WELCOME TO
> THE GREAT DECADES. FELIX

The Youth Cult forces upon us unnatural behavior, phoniness, lies, deceptions, and assorted humiliations.

Working at the Goldwyn Studios in Hollywood a few years ago, I made friends with one of the security officers.

He hurried into my office one morning, breathless and anxious, carrying a small suitcase, and asked if he could use my bathroom.

"Of course," I said.

He looked embarrassed and shamefaced, but finally smiled and said, "I've got to put my corset on."

"Your *what?*"

"Usually I do it at home, but I overslept this morning and I didn't want to take a chance on punching in late. So O.K.?"

"Certainly."

He left the bathroom door open as he changed so that we could continue our conversation. I recall little of it since my astonishment made it impossible to con-

43

centrate. He did indeed take a corset from his suitcase, put it on and lace himself into it cruelly. I then saw him touch up his hair—roots and temples—with a dark-brown eyebrow pencil. Finally, he applied a discreet panchromatic makeup, being careful to include his ears, neck, and the backs of his hands.

Unable to control my curiosity, I blurted out, "What are you *doing*, Jimmy?"

"What I have to."

"Why?"

"Because you don't know, boy," he replied, coming into the office. "You just don't know. The way they're breathin' down my neck around here every day, every minute."

"I don't get it."

"It's like this. I been here so long they've lost track of my age. I been through eight studio managers. So they don't know my records, see? They don't know I'm sixty-seven years of age, or if they do, they forgot. So as long as I can keep from lookin' it, maybe I'm safe. The one thing I couldn't handle right now is a layoff. What with my wife's condition and my boy still institutionalized—maybe forever—and if I should lose *this* job, boy, I'm dead. No chance, no way, nowhere."

We looked at each other for a long time. The man I saw before me was neither resentful nor angry nor improved by cosmetics. He was terrified.

He thanked me and left.

Since that morning, I have often wondered how many of those with whom I have daily dealings may similarly have been forced into such deceptions. I have seen a beautiful actress submit not only to a suc-

cession of face lifts and plastic surgeries, but to sili-
cone injections, with the result that she now appears
to be a hideous, deformed woman of 50, rather than
the serene beauty of 65 which she would have been
had she left herself and nature alone.

In an attempt to deceive others, we end by deceiv-
ing ourselves.

I recall meeting Marie Doro for the first time. She
had been a great Broadway star prior to World War I.
I had never seen her on the stage and did not encoun-
ter her until she was 84. At 84, she was dazzlingly
beautiful and sexually magnetic.

Marilyn Monroe: "I like old people; they have great
qualities younger people don't have. I want to grow
old without face lifts. They take the life out of a face,
the character. I want to have the courage to be loyal
to the face I've made. Sometimes I think it would be
easier to avoid old age, to die young, but then you'd
never complete your life, would you? You'd never
wholly know yourself."

Poor Marilyn. She never got to wholly know herself
—or to grow old.

Youth is Big Business. Youth is for sale in all department stores, in every beauty salon, on far too
many television commercials. They sell; we buy.
Why?

How many men and women have been ripped off
by the purveyors of antiwrinkle creams and lotions
and preparations; or stuff to make eyes brighter, teeth

whiter, hair thicker, bust bigger, stature taller, body thinner or fatter? The billions and billions of dollars spent on these useless, fruitless products might have been spent on something of value.

When Philippe Halsman came to photograph Anna Magnani, he did not want her to be disappointed by his photographs and so warned, "My lens is very sharp, it will show all the lines on your face."

"Don't hide them," she said. "I suffered too much to get them."

The noted New York plastic surgeon, Dr. Blair Rogers, looking over his daily schedule, saw that it listed ten patients, and said, "I'd say at least six of these patients are having the surgery for purely economic reasons. Take a fairly typical kind of patient I see, a lady in her fifties whose husband has died recently. She has a couple of kids in college. Suddenly, she's no longer a housewife. She *has* to work. So she goes looking for a job as a receptionist or a secretary. She may be a wonderful person, but to an employment manager, she looks like an old lady. Cosmetic surgery can make her employable."

In her seventies, Marlene Dietrich continued to draw sell-out houses everywhere in the world. She said: "They don't come to see me just because I take the trouble to look as good as I can. They come because I represent something—courage, stamina, faith, motherhood, who knows? Sometimes they just sit there in stunned silence, amazed that I'm still alive and moving."

*How old would you be if you didn't know
how old you was?*

Satchel Paige

I would like to tell the story of my tooth, not because I am tooth-proud, but because Dr. Leonard Hirschfeld, my periodontist, assures me that it is a significant, scientifically important Right Upper Lateral Incisor.

He first encountered it some thirty years ago. It had been long neglected as a result of my extended period of service in the Army of the United States, during which I feared to submit to Army dental care. Upon my discharge, the tooth was in bad shape. My dentist decided it should be extracted and replaced. He sent me to an exodontist, who prepared to separate me from my far-gone tooth.

At the last moment, he leaned in for a closer look, then said, "Doggone, I hate to extract a front tooth. It always leads to trouble. Would you be willing to spend a little time and effort to find out if it could possibly be saved? Mind you, I don't think it can be, but just on the chance? We can always pull it next week."

"Sure," I said, although I was disappointed, having psyched myself up for the depressing event.

"O.K.," he said. "Go see the Hirschfelds. They're father and son and nobody better."

A few days later, father and son were tapping that tooth and becoming excited by the challenge:

"If you want to try," said Dr. Isidore Hirschfeld, the father, "we can try, but don't expect miracles."

"Don't listen to him," said Dr. Leonard Hirschfeld, the son. "*Expect* miracles."

So it began. A year or more of visits during which that dying tooth hung by a thread—literally and figuratively—while Dr. Leonard Hirschfeld worked to revive it.

Time passed, the great Dr. Isidore died, but my tooth lived on.

I do not know precisely what was done other than the application of progressive and creative science, but the tooth still lives some thirty years later and serves me well each day.

Dr. Leonard Hirschfeld tells me that a record of its history—with photographs—has been published in his textbook *Minor Tooth Movement in General Practice*, and is used as part of his course at Columbia University.

I include this account because it seems germane. The conventional thing would have been to pull the tooth and let it go, but all through my late thirties, my forties and fifties and even into my sixties, it has flourished and developed in the same way that stubble appears on my chin each morning, and that my fingernails grow constantly, as if to remind me that I, too, am still growing daily.

The life force continues in curious but clear ways.

We are asked to believe that life in our time is the exclusive province of the Young; that only young people are attractive, and even in that mold, certain standards are official. A uniform concept of the attractive man, a single perception of a beautiful woman.

The facts of nature do not support this view. Everyone is, or can be, attractive to someone. Cases differ, and the eye of the beholder is infinitely varied: "What does she see in him?" "What does he see in her?"

At the time when breast fetish was sweeping the world of fashion, when falsies became an industry, when cleavage was definitely "in," there appeared on the scene a knockout named Audrey Hepburn. Slim, incandescent, gifted, and small-breasted.

Preparing to make her first important film, she was shocked by the suggestion that she wear pads in her brassière.

"It's ridiculous," she protested, "they'll put me out of proportion." The argument continued. Studio pressure was applied, but Audrey Hepburn could not be persuaded.

"They say my neck is too long, and perhaps it is," she said. "Do you expect me to shorten it?"

Fortunately for her and for her career, she prevailed and went on in her own person and with her own body to become one of the great film stars of her time.

"Audrey Hepburn," observed the waggish Billy Wilder, "has put bosoms back forty years!"

Before leaving (reluctantly) the subject of Audrey Hepburn, it is interesting to consider subsequent developments. She retired from the screen for eight years. When she returned, we were astounded by the transformation. She had left as a lovely young gazelle;

a splendid, charming girl. When she returned, she had become a woman—deep, and rich, and irresistible. She had not aged, she had matured. No longer sparkling champagne, now she was a rare vintage wine. We drank her in, and the results were heady.

Discussing her new status, she said, "Well, I *am* forty-seven, and I think it's silly to play younger parts. People have been youth worshipers too long."

When asked if a woman could age in a beautiful and interesting way, she laughed and said, "We've *got* to believe that! Otherwise, what would you do—shoot yourself?

"Of course, one would love to be younger—to have more time. Yet there's a big advantage in being older. Since you've done a lot of things you feel you *have* to do, there's a luxury in being able to retire before it's time to retire . . . do you know what I mean?

"We're all aware of time passing, but with me it's more subconscious. It's not just getting older or having gray hair or whatever. It's death, but also it's the possible absence of being loved. I think I'd never worry about age if I knew I could go on being loved and having the possibility to love. . . . I think it's one of the great tragedies in this world—the old who are lonely. So it isn't age or even death that one fears, as much as loneliness and the lack of affection."

The extraordinary customs inspector/painter Henri Rousseau, at 65, fell in love with a woman in his village. She was 59. Her father, 83, objected strenuously to the idea of their marriage. Rousseau wrote him:

One can still be in love at my age without being ridiculous. It's not the same sort of love that young people go in for, but must one resign oneself to living alone just because one's old? It's dreadful going back to lonely lodgings. It's at my age that one most needs one's heart warmed up again. . . . It's not right to laugh at old people who get married again; you need the company of someone you love. . . .

And here is another love story:

In 1915, Rose Kohansky and George Halagowski were teenagers living on the same block in Rahway, New Jersey. They dated steadily and talked of marriage. Then the United States entered World War I. George joined the infantry and went overseas. The long separation shattered their romance, and by the time George returned, Rose had married someone else. They did not see each other for the next fifty-seven years. Then, quite by accident, they met. They were both 74 now, with grandchildren and great-grandchildren. Still, this did not deter them from rekindling what they had had in the past. They were married at St. Mark's Catholic Church in Bayonne. Together they furnished an apartment and went off on a ten-week honeymoon in Spain.

"It's like being young again," said the newlywed Mrs. Halagowski.

"Men and women," said my friend the actuary, "if they are normal—want to live. It's the only way we can explain the constantly rising figure of life expectancy. If you look at the graph for the past two hundred years, the rise is absolutely steady—up up up every year, and there's no reason to expect that this trend is ever going to change. The more man learns about himself and his world, the better he's able to look after himself, protect himself, preserve himself. A hundred years ago: life span in the 40's. Today, in the 70's. All right, then. In *another* hundred years, it'll be in the 90's; and by the Quadricentennial, in the 120's. Why not? What's to stop it? If it hasn't been stopped by now, it's not going to be. Our air quality is worse than it has ever been, our water is poisoned, our foods are more and more adulterated. 'The Surgeon General has determined that cigarette smoking is dangerous to your health'—that is what it says on every pack, and still millions of people smoke billions of cigarettes. Also, you see a growing consumption of coffee and alcohol. We take drugs and eat carelessly and yet . . . that life expectancy figure just keeps rising. It can't be explained scientifically. Maybe it's what Shaw used to call the 'Life Force.' It seems to gain power forever, rooted in the basic desire to live a long time."

If all this is true, a revolutionary reversal in our thinking about youth and age will have to take place. If men are to be retired at 50, and then live to 90, some thought will have to be given to that important forty-year span.

A preoccupation with the new, the fresh, the shiny, the up-to-date, pervades our thinking and living.

In the automobile-oriented society of Southern California the growing fashion is to acquire each year's new model by trading in last year's, creating, on the one hand, a continuum of debt; but, on the other hand, always a brand-new model in the garage.

Time was when an automobile served its owner for several years, sometimes as many as ten or even twenty, but all that, as we know, has changed.

A story is told of how this system came about. An executive of one of the major automobile manufacturers of Michigan was in the habit of making an annual trip to Paris with his wife. Both were Francophiles, spoke the language, loved the land and its people, its food and wine.

On one trip, the wife announced that she might have to stay an additional week because the new wardrobes she had ordered from Chanel, Dior, and Balenciaga would not be ready until that time.

"What do you mean, new wardrobes?" asked the bemused executive.

"Why, this year's," replied his wife.

"What happened to *last* year's?"

"What *are* you talking about?" she responded impatiently. "*Last* year's was *last* year's. I can't wear *those*, can I?"

"Why not?"

She regarded him as though he were a backward child as she said, "Because they're *last* year's, dear."

"Oh," he said.

The next morning, when his wife went off to her fittings, he went for his customary walk in the Bois de Boulogne and as he walked, he thought. "No wonder this fashion business is so immense. They've fixed it so that their customers have to buy a new wardrobe every year. How do they do it? They do it by changing the fashion every year. So each year—new dresses, new lengths, new hats, new colors." Then it struck him: "Couldn't this whimsical notion be transferred to the automobile industry? Couldn't we fix it so that *automobiles* went out of style every year or every couple years?" Eureka!

When he returned to Detroit, he began a series of secret meetings with his sales, advertising, and public relations departments. A few behavioral scientists were brought in as consultants.

The following year, without fanfare, or overt signs, the plan was put into effect and has continued to the present day.

In a nation of status-seekers, it is not difficult to sell a new model every year.

By the same token, older people, along with older cars, are considered out of fashion, obsolete—but it is all a fraud, a trick, a result of sick thinking.

> *The fact that for the last 15 or 20 years of*
> *his life a man should be no more than a re-*
> *ject, a piece of scrap, reveals the failure of*
> *our civilization.*
>
> *Simone de Beauvoir*

Picasso was once asked if standing before his easel five or six hours at a stretch did not tire him.

"No," he said. "That is why painters live so long. While I work, I leave my body outside the door, the way Muslims take off their shoes before entering the mosque."

It is true that there are some activities that can be pursued more effectively and efficiently in youth. By the same token, there are others that require long practice and experience, that can be acquired only with passing years.

My sister-in-law, about to undergo surgery, was advised by her internist to "get a young man to do it." She demurred, since she had complete faith in her own man, a distinguished surgeon, aged 62.

"What's wrong with Ben?" she asked.

"Well, he's pretty old," was the response. "Sixty-two and after all, let's face it, at sixty-two, the hands aren't so steady and the reflexes aren't so good. No. Get a young man."

When she asked for my opinion, I replied, "Well, let's put it this way: If I had to have a brain tumor removed, and they said to me, 'Now you've got your choice. Dr. A, who's eighty-two years old and richly experienced in such matters. In fact, last Wednesday, he removed seven in one day. Or if you prefer, you can have Dr. B, who's said to be the most brilliant young man to come out of Harvard Medical School in years. He's twenty-two years old and he's itching to get at your brain tumor.' Well, you can imagine how long it would take me to make *that* decision."

She went with the old man, who performed the necessary surgery as he had done thousands of times before, swiftly, effectively, and successfully.

While the decision was still in the balance, and my hapless relative was being bombarded with advice from all sides, I attended one of Arthur Rubinstein's recitals at Carnegie Hall.

Precisely at the announced hour, the old master strode onto the stage. He accepted the ovation with his customary grace, yet somehow conveyed that he wished it to end in order that he might get on with the business of the afternoon, which was to play the piano. He began, and as he went on, going from strength to strength, piling astonishment upon astonishment, thrilling his audience with his technical mastery, and moving it deeply with his emphatic feeling, I could not help but relate the event to our family problem, because here was Rubinstein, in his ninetieth—yes, ninetieth!—year, playing better than ever before. A powerful man at the dizzying peak of his immortal powers.

Leaving aside any consideration of talent, genius, taste, judgment, spirit, experience, emotion, passion, nuance, wisdom, elegance—that is to say, the abstracts—I considered the purely physical requirements of what was taking place before my eyes and ears. Playing the piano involves the accurate manipulation of eighty-eight keys with ten fingers, and two pedals with two feet. In the course of his recital, Rubinstein was called upon to play some three million notes. A pianist of his stature is permitted no errors, and indeed, he made none.

Why, I wondered, are the skills of a surgeon, handling scalpel and sutures, any more demanding than those that Rubinstein was demonstrating so supremely?

I left the hall with the conviction that practice and repetition and experience and judgment can be more important than the raw bursting energies of youth.

Pablo Casals was another wise man who turned his back on the warning finger of age. "As long as one can admire and love," he said, "then one is young forever."

> *The youth gets together materials for a bridge to the moon and at length a middle-aged man decides to build a woodshed of them.*
>
> *Henry David Thoreau*

In a time when an American man's life expectancy was 33, Benjamin Franklin, that most civilized of beings, lived to be 84.

His life in Colonial America was hard. He survived blistering summers and punishing winters. Traveling, which he did as much as any man of his time, was physically debilitating. A trip from Boston to Philadelphia took three difficult days of coach travel. Even the distance from Philadelphia to New York occupied a long day. His many trips abroad were wearing. To London and return, to Paris and return, again and again, each journey lasting from five to seven weeks.

The range of his interests and activities is impressive, even to the modern man. Printer, publisher, author, humorist, statesman, scientist, inventor, innovator (adult education, life insurance, *The Saturday Evening Post*, the Franklin stove), ambassador, signer of the Declaration of Independence.

At 80, Franklin invented the flexible catheter, experimented with treatment of paralysis by electricity, and did significant work on lead poisoning. He also concerned himself with the alleviation of gout, insomnia, fever, deafness, the common cold, infection from dead bodies, and the death rate of infants.

Further, at about this time, he became increasingly irritated by the deterioration of his eyes. He thought it a nuisance to have to use two pairs of glasses: one for distance, another for reading. Many had been similarly bothered. But Benjamin Franklin invented bifocal lenses.

He once remarked that all want to live long but that none want to be old.

One of the advantages of *this* century is the growing recognition not only that senior citizens should not be discarded but that they can be valuable resources.

Certain of Franklin's biographers have marveled at his longevity in the face of the range of his activities and its correlative expenditure of energy. They miss the point. Franklin's life span was achieved not in *spite* of this vivacity, but *because* of it. Active people learn in time that it is the functions of their existence which generate energy.

The battery of an unused automobile that stands in a garage for several weeks will almost invariably run down. The running car charges its battery. Energy in physics and in nature is generated by action, by movement: a windmill, a waterfall, a dynamo—whatever is the opposite of stagnation.

Lou Brock, a baseball phenomenon at 38, says: "Once you're in shape, you have a tendency to stay that way. To get *out* of shape, you have to *work* at it."

In many respects, man is a machine. Franklin—

the scientist, the philosopher—understood this. He lived by rules, by maxims. He organized his time frugally, meting out the hours with care and consideration. See him sitting there stark naked before an open window at the beginning of each of his mornings, "ordering the day," as he put it.

"Don't waste time," he once said. "That's the stuff life's made of."

In his fortieth year, he composed the letter which has become one of the most celebrated of his writings. A troubled young friend had written him asking for advice on the subject of marriage. Herewith, Franklin's reply:

June 25, 1745

My Dear Friend:—

I know of no Medicine fit to diminish the violent and natural inclination you mention; and if I did, I think I should not communicate it to you. Marriage is the proper Remedy. It is the most natural State of Man, and therefore the State in which you will find solid Happiness. Your Reason against entering into it at present appears to be not well founded. The Circumstantial Advantages you have in View by Postponing it, are not only uncertain, but they are small in comparison with the Thing itself, *the being married and settled*. It is the Man and Woman united that makes the complete human Being. Separate she wants his force of Body and Strength of Reason; he her

Softness, Sensibility and acute Discernment. Together they are most likely to succeed in the World. A single Man has not nearly the Value he would have in that State of Union. He is an incomplete Animal. He resembles the odd Half of a Pair of Scissors.

If you get a prudent, healthy wife, your Industry in your Profession, with her good Economy, will be a Fortune sufficient.

But if you will not take this Counsel, and persist in thinking a Commerce with the Sex is inevitable, then I repeat my former Advice that in your Amours you should *prefer old Women to young ones*. This you call a Paradox, and demand my reasons. They are these:

1 Because they have more Knowledge of the world and their Minds are better stored with Observations; their Conversation is more improving, and more lastingly agreeable.

2 Because when Women cease to be handsome, they study to be good. To maintain their Influence over Man, they supply the Diminution of Beauty by an Augmentation of Utility. They learn to do a thousand Services, small and great, and are the most tender and useful of all Friends when you are sick. Thus they continue amiable. And hence there is hardly such a thing to be found as an old Woman who is not a good Woman.

3 Because there is no hazard of children, which irregularly produced may be attended with much inconvenience.

4 Because through more Experience they are more prudent and discreet in conducting an Intrigue to prevent Suspicion. The Commerce with them is therefore safer with regard to your reputation; and with regard to theirs, if the Affair should happen to be known, considerate People might be inclined to excuse an old Woman, who would kindly take care of a young Man, form his manners by her good Councils, and prevent his ruining his Health and Fortune among mercinary Prostitutes.

5 Because in every Animal that walks upright, the Deficiency of the Fluids that fill the Muscles appears first in the highest Part. The Face first grows lank and wrinkled; then the Neck; then the Breast and Arms; the lower parts continuing to the last as plump as ever; so that covering all above with a Basket, and regarding only what is below the Girdle, it is impossible of two Women to know an old from a young one. And as in the Dark all Cats are at least equal and frequently superior; every Knack being by Practice capable of improvement.

6 Because the sin is less. The Debauching of a Virgin may be her Ruin, and make her for Life unhappy.

7 Because the Compunction is less. The

having made a young Girl *miserable* may give you frequent and bitter Reflections; none of which can attend making an old Woman *happy*.

8th & lastly. They are so grateful!!!

Thus much for my Paradox. But still I advise you to marry immediately; being sincerely

Your Affectionate Friend,
Benj. Franklin

Men who have foolishly accepted the myth of middle-age fading sexual interest would do well to make a study of the last twenty years of Dr. Franklin's life. It was during this period that his well-known secret affair with the beautiful Madame Helvétius took place, and it is to that indiscreet lady's detailed report that we owe our knowledge of Franklin's undiminished virility.

She was the most distinguished *salonnière* of her day; the remarkable, much-desired woman to whom Fontenelle, at 100, said, "Ah, my dear, if only I were ninety again!"

She was 60 and Franklin in his mid-seventies when they shared their great romance. Once, when she scolded him for having put off a promised visit, Franklin said, "Madame, I am waiting till the nights are longer." He was a highly adaptable man who was able to pick up the manners and morals of whatever time and place he occupied. The free-swinging, pre-Revolutionary gaiety of France suited his temperament perfectly.

There is, of course, no complete historical record of his dalliances, but it was not only the *on dit,* it was common knowledge that he was a man of many pleasures.

Letters survive to record his love affair with Madame Brillon. In England, Polly Hewson and Georgiana Shipley were the last of his conquests. In his eighties, as in his thirties, he fathered an unrecorded number of illegitimate offspring.

It can be argued that Benjamin Franklin was a phenomenon, a genius, a *lusus naturae,* and that ordinary mortals cannot aspire to the emulation of such a giant. But they can and should. The great men and women are the ones who surpass the standards, who expand human possibility.

Consider what Helen Keller, setting an example, has done for generations of blind or deaf children and their parents; what Franklin Roosevelt did to inspire thousands upon thousands of the handicapped.

Certainly we should all attempt to imitate Franklin —that "harmonious human multitude"—and even dream of besting him. We shall probably fail, but in the attempt, in the struggle, we may produce the energy and create the excitement that make life at any age worth living.

You're only young once—and if you work it
right—once is enough!

Joe E. Lewis

The case of the *Commonwealth of Massachusetts* v. *Robert D. Murgia* came before the Supreme Court of the United States during the October term of 1974.

Murgia's lawyers presented the same arguments they had used before the District Court and added others.

They contended that age, like sex, was merely an accident of birth; and like sex, often bore no relation to the ability to perform or to contribute to society.

They insisted that distinctions based upon age, like those based upon sex, were grounded in a series of misconceptions that have come to pervade the statute books and that have the effect of relegating older people to an inferior status regardless of *individual ability*. They asked the Court to scrutinize carefully such age-based classifications in the same way they had considered gender-based classifications.

And they presented the overwhelming medical evidence against the Massachusetts statute.

They offered documents and studies which proved that older people displaced from their jobs were faced

67

not only with severe economic and physical stresses, but with dangerous psychological effects. They reminded the Court that older people who were fired or forcibly retired found it difficult, if not impossible, to find new employment. They offered charts showing that pensions, benefits, and other substitute sources of income were not adequate to maintain a fair living standard.

In a final passionate argument, they stated that the Older Americans Act of 1965 declared it to be the duty of government to assist older people in securing equal opportunity for employment, with no discriminatory personnel practices because of age. They maintained that governmental agencies are under specific instructions from the President of the United States to eliminate age discrimination in the Federal Government, adding that thirty states have specific legislation forbidding discrimination based on age—*including* Massachusetts. The Massachusetts General Laws declare it to be against public policy to dismiss from employment any person between the ages of 45 and 65 on the basis of age. This statute has been held to be equal to a criminal statute.

Along with their case, they submitted an *amicus curiae* brief filed by the American Medical Association, which stated in part:

> It is the position of the American Medical Association that the nation's social policy for the aging should ensure that middle aged and older workers have the opportunity to continue in productive employment as long as they wish and are able physically, men-

tally, and medically to maintain the appropriate level of job efficiency. Such opportunities will enable many more middle aged and older people to look forward to more years of independence, dignity, and usefulness. . . .

For society, the failure to use the wisdom, experience and productivity of middle aged and older persons creates voids that may be filled by those less capable. Instead of using proficient middled aged and older people, society sets up special agencies to care for them in their dependency, then spends more funds to train new younger workers. These losses could be reduced if middle aged and older persons had more opportunities to remain productive. . . .

In the opinion of the American Medical Association, any decision for or against retirement should rest on the same fundamentals as does a decision for or against hiring: (1) the individual's desire to work; and (2) the individual's ability to work.

Chronological age has been observed to have no magic in terms of judgment, ability, and physical dexterity. Individuals may lose these qualities at age 40 or retain them past age 80. The granting and continuance of employment opportunities should be based on the individual's competence and ability—not his age. . . .

Man's increasing life expectancy will

prove of little use to him if at an arbitrary age he is denied the right to work and produce. Further, if he is forced into idleness, it is questionable whether our society can survive the financial burden of larger numbers of dependent persons. Our society and economy need the productive contributions that middle aged and older persons can make.

Another *amici* brief was filed by the American Association of Retired Persons, the National Retired Teachers Association, and the National Senior Citizens Law Center. Among other things, it said:

Work is one of the most important aspects of human existence and the freedom to work is an interest of constitutional dimensions. . . . The practical effect of involuntary retirement, for most people, is loss of the means for gainful employment; alternative job opportunities are, as a practical matter, non-existent. . . . Obviously, an individual must work to eat and thus freedom to work is the cornerstone of life itself.

Supplementing the American Medical Association's *amicus curiae*, Dr. Frederick C. Swartz, the Chairman of its Committee on Aging, submitted a supportive paper. He wrote:

The increase in life expectancy and higher health levels will prove of little benefit to man if he is denied the opportunity to continue contributing of his skills at a certain chronological age, whether this be 45, 65, or 85 years. . . .

From the beginning of life until its end, these objectives and motivations should continue to apply. Unfortunately, however, they apply only until a certain chronological age —most often 65—when forces outside of medicine inflict a disease—or disability-producing condition upon working men and women that is no less devastating than cancer, tuberculosis, or heart disease. This condition—enforced idleness—robs those afflicted of the will to live full, well-rounded lives, deprives them of opportunities for compelling physical and mental activity, and encourages atrophy and decay.

This condition has brainwashed thousands into the belief that at 65 one is over the hill. It has imposed the philosophy of the marketplace on the employee—a philosophy that substitutes the concept "Throw out all of the old and defective" for the dictum "To do good and to do no harm."

In addition, a completely new point was raised: Massachusetts set the age for compulsory retirement of State Policemen at age 50 in 1939, when longevity was statistically shorter. In 1920, for example, ten years after a Massachusetts mandatory retirement system was established, the expected life span was 54.

But by 1940, only one year after 50 was set by Massachusetts as the mandatory retirement age for State Policemen, the expected life span had risen from 54 to 63. By 1972, it had jumped to 71. Despite these dramatic changes and the absence of any evidence supporting the maintenance of the standards of another generation, Massachusetts' mandatory retirement of its State Policemen at 50 remains unaltered.

Finally, an *amici* brief was filed by the American Civil Liberties Union, the National Council of Senior Citizens, and the Massachusetts Civil Liberties Union.

The American Civil Liberties Union repeated its long-standing principle that "The test for employment should be the ability of the individual to perform the particular job function."

It asked:

> Are older people "subjected to a history of purposeful unequal treatment?" Clearly yes. That history is perhaps not a long one: in the 19th century and before, few people attained 65 years of age, and those who did were productive members of society. . . . But the history of the 20th century is one of increasing prejudice and prejudicial treatment, exemplified by the expansion of our mandatory policies and statutes. Presumably, it might be suggested that one must wait for 300 years of discrimination, such as Blacks have experienced, before the "history of purposeful unequal treatment" rises to constitutional significance.

The ACLU concluded by quoting Emerson:

> "A man's years should not be counted
> until he has nothing else to count." . . .
>
> If the marks of individual integrity and
> happiness, and of society's treatment of its
> members, are to be measured for the older
> man and woman in this nation, the conclu-
> sion must be that ours is a nation sadly at
> odds with itself. We exalt youth, and de-
> mean old age. We commend productivity
> and creativity, and then cut off those who
> are still able to produce and to create. We
> deplore poverty, and condemn the old to its
> ravages. We mouth respect for the individ-
> ual, and use pernicious generalizations to
> victimize the many.

The Commonwealth of Massachusetts had a
different view of the Murgia case and presented it
forcefully before the Supreme Court.

It based its case upon the right of the Commonwealth to establish such a statute. The consistently
threatening bugaboo of states' rights was raised with
the knowledge that it had frequently vexed the High
Court.

The Commonwealth reached back into 1914 to
quote a commission on pensions:

> It would undoubtedly be most advantageous
> to the individual and most beneficial to the
> public service if each case could be treated
> entirely on its merit as to the time when the

employee should be retired. The execution of such a plan among a large number of employees, however, offers obstacles which are well-nigh insurmountable.

Leaning on this hoary argument—that people cannot be dealt with individually—the Commonwealth then stated:

Essentially, state and federal legislatures have chosen to avoid the depressing and demeaning task of determining, on a case-by-case basis, when an individual has reached an elusive point of diminished productivity.

Who was it said, "Beware lest the living come to be governed by the dead"?

You can teach an old dog new tricks.

Anon.

A recent report by the National Housing Authority is disquieting.

It recommends a reorganization in the planning of low-cost housing since it has been found that the old and the young cannot live side by side harmoniously. In projects where the elderly are in a minority, the crime rate has ballooned dangerously.

Older people are easy marks for muggings, holdups, burglaries, robberies, and purely mischievous attacks by young people who share the current lack of respect for the old.

Generalization, although convenient for purposes of discussion, is dangerous.

It is not possible to state with accuracy that: "Young people are . . ."; "Elderly people want . . ."; "Retirees must . . .".

There are always exceptions, many of them inspiring. Consider the case of Michael Mirakian, Coordinator of Student Affairs at the Robert Taft High School in the Bronx.

Appalled by the increasing number of assaults on and harassments of older people in the neighborhood

75

of the school, Mirakian organized over two hundred of his students into a volunteer force whose activity is to escort and protect senior citizens on shopping trips, walks, visits to doctors and dentists, and the like.

The plan is working. Crimes against the elderly in the area have been reduced to virtually zero. In more civilized societies, the old and the young complement one another comfortably and happily.

Another heartening breakthrough of the wall that often separates the generations took place in California. Three young Stanford students, Jon Else, Kristine Samuelson, and Steven Kovacs, made a half-hour documentary film titled *Arthur and Lillie*, and won the 1976 Golden Gate Award at the San Francisco Film Festival. Its subjects? Arthur Mayer, 89, and his wife, Lillie, 86.

Arthur Mayer was an important figure in the film industry for many years, owned theatres and a distribution company. At 75, he retired and almost immediately suffered illness and depression.

Fortunately, he was invited to help organize a film department at Brandeis University. He says, "They thought I was *Louis B.* Mayer and would endow it." In any event, he went to work and did the job. This led to offers from other universities. He found himself teaching film at Dartmouth, USC, UCLA, Stanford, and NYU. For almost fifteen years, he has been busier than ever before and his plans for the future include many things, but not retirement.

Forty-five per cent of the murders in the United States are committed by people under 25. Seventy-five per cent of *all* crime is committed by people under 30.

Surely the young have a great deal to gain, practically and inspirationally, from their elders. Conversely, older people who have younger ones in their lives profit by the association.

Eliot Wigginton, an educational M.A. from Cornell University, went to Rabun Gap, Georgia, in the Appalachians to teach ninth- and tenth-grade high school. He had a difficult time, being unable to communicate with his strange, unruly students. The absence of rapport reached clinical proportions.

In desperation, he put aside the curriculum and decided to let the students publish a magazine about things that interested them.

Collectively, they chose a name for the magazine—*Foxfire*, after a tiny organism that glows in the dark and is often seen in the mountain coves.

The kids went out, talked to people in the area and brought back stories about superstitions, old home remedies, weather signs, a story about a hog hunt, a taped interview with the retired sheriff about the time the local bank was robbed, and directions for planting by the signs of the zodiac.

They scrounged around, managed to get together $450 to finance the printing of the first issue. The six hundred copies sold out in a week. They printed six hundred more. In time, the first volume of *Foxfire*, published in 1972, sold over a million copies. It was followed by *Foxfire 2* and *Foxfire 3*.

Eliot Wigginton thinks *Foxfire*'s success can be duplicated elsewhere.

"Daily, our grandparents are moving out of our lives, taking with them irreparably the kind of information contained in this book. They are taking it, not because they want to, but because they think we don't care. And it isn't happening just in Appalachia. I think, for example, of numerous Indian reservations, Black cultures near the Southern coast, Ozark Mountain communities and a hundred others."

Eliot Wigginton believes if one can bridge the gap between the neglected elderly and the apathetic young, he will have contributed to progress. He has.

Why not aim for a complete integration of our society, not only racial and religious, but embracing *all* segments and classifications? Our social power derives from the extent to which we are able to integrate such diverse elements as North and South, labor and management, rich and poor, young and old. The greatest progress in civilization has been achieved *not* by competition, but by cooperation.

For the young man is handsome, but the old superb. . . . Fire is seen in the eyes of the young, but it is light that we see in the old man's eyes.

Victor Hugo

We return to the practical truth that age *is* largely a matter of attitude.

Not long ago, I was preparing to direct a play entitled *Ho! Ho! Ho!*, written by my wife. For an important role in the second act, I needed an elderly actor to play the part of a volatile, energetic, old Yankee. Some of my favorite players of the past had retired and were reluctant to leave the comforts of California or Florida, and two turned me down. Then I remembered an old actor who, several years ago, had played an effective bit in a film I had directed in New York. I could not remember his name, but I did recall that he had lived at The Lambs. Alas, The Lambs clubhouse was no more, and I wondered if perhaps he, too, had failed to survive. After a long search, I found his name—James O'Neill. With some trepidation, I phoned the membership department of Actors Equity Association and inquired.

"James O'Neill?" was the response. "Sure, Hotel Royalton."

They seemed to know him at once, which indicated he was still active. I phoned him and asked him to come in and see me. A day later, in came a tall, attractive, hale gentleman, beautifully dressed for summer with a little straw hat jauntily perched on his headful of white hair.

We chatted for a time. I gave him a copy of the play, asked him to read it at his convenience and to return when he had done so.

Two hours later he was back. He discussed the play and the part more trenchantly than any other player had done up to that point. He impressed me with subtle insights that had escaped me even though I had been studying the play for more than a year.

I asked him if he was interested and available.

"Yes," he said.

"Well, then—I'd like you to do it."

He opened the script to the page on which his entrance was indicated and stood up.

"What're you doing?" I asked.

"Why, don't you want me to read for you?"

"No, I'd just like you to go to the producer's office and sign your contract."

"Oh," he said, surprised. "Very well."

"And don't worry about the song," I said. "It may be in or out."

"That's not a worry," he said. "I was the second Finian in *Finian's Rainbow*." Whereupon, he sang a chorus of "How Are Things in Glocca Morra?" with great charm and effect.

"That's fine."

Preparing to leave, he asked, "Aren't you a member of The Players?"

"Yes, I am."

"I don't seem to see you much down there."

"I know. I love The Players, but it's such a long trip to Gramercy Park. I hardly ever have the time."

"Well," he said, "I usually walk down. It makes for a nice walk."

He started out the door, sticking his hat on his head at a rakish angle. He stopped, looked at me oddly, and asked, "Don't you want to know how old I am?"

"No. Why would I?"

"I don't know. Usually, when I tell people what I've done, they want to know how old I am."

"*I* don't."

"Oh."

He seemed disappointed, so I said, "But if you want to tell me, tell me."

He brightened. "I'm ninety-two!"

I was overwhelmed.

"That's right. I played my first part on the professional stage on April 10, 1888, and I'm still going strong."

"You certainly are."

On his ninetieth birthday, the American poet John Hall Wheelock said, "I've always wanted to live long. I had a lot of work I wanted to do. In old age, things become more intense rather than less so. Things get more poignant—so many associations—everything reverberating with everything else. You don't feel you are any older, but suddenly you realize you are. But instead of life getting dimmer and duller, it gets so poignant, it's unbearable. Like looking at the sun, you can't stand it because it's unbearable."

As the great Goya continued to work well into old age, he observed that it was his struggle toward perfection that provided a constant renewal of his energy and imagination. Baudelaire was impressed by Goya's creativity toward the end of his life: "At the end of his career, Goya's sight had failed to such a degree that it is said he had to have his pencils sharpened for him. Yet even at that period he carried out very large and important lithographs, splendid plates that are immense pictures in miniature—a fresh piece of evidence in support of that strange law ruling the fate of great artists, a law which lays down that their lives and intelligences should run in opposite directions, that what they lose on the one hand, they should gain on the other, and that they should thus go on in a continual youth, gathering fresh strength, new spirit and even greater daring right up until the very edge of the grave."

Students of the life and work of Voltaire are agreed that his old age increased the power of his concentration, the vitality of his efforts, and the glories of his achievements.

1966. Cannes. A Pablo Picasso retrospective—dazzling—is in progress. Hundreds of canvases, meticulously arranged in chronological order, line the walls. As one enters, the first works to be seen are those of the callow, adolescent beginner; conventional landscapes and still lifes. A little farther on, the landscapes change, take on new colors. The still lifes become less still. An artist is finding his voice. Turning the corner, one comes upon bold experiments, cubism, acrobats, erotic drawings. Freer and ever freer the spirit, culminating in an explosion of never-before-seen colors and shapes and visions.

The viewers are visibly impressed by the rare exhibition. How often is the long life of one man's perception displayed on one day in a single gallery?

Through it all, Picasso himself moves, enjoying the show more than anyone. He wears red velvet trousers, an Italian silk green jacket, a French sailor's matelot, and on his great head—incongruous but perfect—a Swiss Alpine hat with feather. He is smoking, bubbling, laughing. He is 85. Two luscious young girls are his companions.

A handsome woman approaches him. A friend. He kisses her hand. They embrace, then he kisses her properly.

"Maître!" she cries. "It is formidable! Stupendous!"

"Yes, yes," says the master.

"But I do not understand the grouping, not at all."

"How so?"

"Well, the beginning pictures—over there—so mature, so serious and solemn—then the later ones, more and more different and wild. It is almost as if the dates should be reversed. Starting here with your new works and ending there with the first. How do you explain it?"

83

"Easily," replies Picasso, his eyes sparkling. "It takes a long time to become young!"

Impulsively, he seizes his old friend and kisses her again.

> *It is possible to be youthful at any age, except when you're young.*
>
> Samuel Vaughan

"Senior citizens" is an unfortunate appellation for the group it describes. So bland, so meaningless.

Adele Astaire, entrancing at 81, says, "Please don't call me a senior citizen. I hate that. If you have to call me something, I prefer 'old bag.'"

Many of the older people in our world are valuable not because they are senior, but because they are experienced. Consider the recent instance of E. B. White and the Xerox Corporation. Mr. White, to whom we are indebted for some of the most stylish prose in our language, has lived for forty years in North Brooklin, Maine, while continuing to be one of *The New Yorker*'s principal contributors.

In February 1976, something unprecedented occurred in the literary world. *Esquire* published an article by Harrison E. Salisbury. It had been commissioned and paid for by the Xerox Corporation.

It may be that many who saw it were troubled by the direction this practice might take, but only E. B. White acted.

He wrote a letter to *The Ellsworth American*, published in Brooklin, Maine (circulation 3,232), and closed by saying:

> Well, it doesn't take a great intellectual to detect in all this the shadow of disaster. If magazines decide to farm out their writers to advertisers, and accept the advertiser's payment to the writer, and to the magazine, then the periodicals of this country will be far down the drain, and will become so fuzzy as to be indistinguishable from the controlled press in other parts of the world.

Why he did not write to *The New York Times;* or use his own forum, *The New Yorker;* or write directly to the Xerox Corporation is a question only he can answer. No matter. His letter came to the attention of the Xerox Corporation, and a correspondence ensued.

W. B. Jones of Xerox began by writing White that as a long-time admirer of his work, and as one of the instigators of the *Esquire* arrangement, he had read White's letter with some dismay. He explained that Xerox had viewed the sponsorship as an extension of its backing of television programs, "which were never about our business in any way; in some cases, they were so controversial that customers tossed out their Xerox machines."

White entered into an eloquent exchange with various members of the Xerox Corporation.

Finally, David J. Curtin, Vice President, Communications, for Xerox, announced that they were abandoning the entire project. Speaking of E. B. White, he said, "He stopped us in our tracks. We have enormous respect for Mr. White and if this was un-settling to him, it was just not worth continuing it."

E. B. White said, "I was a little surprised. When you get to be as big a corporation as that, you don't have to listen to a little fellow like me."

The poisonous, dangerous, spreading weed had been effectively nipped in the bud—not by a union, not by an organization, not by another corporation, but by one small man who knew what had to be done and who did it. His age? Seventy-six.

Where were the rest of us?

Certainly there are many intelligent, honest, far-seeing young men presently employed in publishing. Where were their voices? Where were the 20-year-old students of journalism, the 30-year-old investigative reporters, the 40-year-old editors, the 50-year-old crit-ics, the 60-year-old lawyers? How is it that it took a 76-year-old writer, living way up in North Brooklin, Maine, to raise his voice and accomplish the deed?

Experience. Precedent. The long view.

The case is not so much against the derelict younger people as it is *for* E. B. White. At the crucial moment, a man with wisdom and vision was available.

A young songwriter, talking to Oscar Hammerstein, was foolishly putting down the work of Irving Berlin.

"'All alone/By the telephone,'" he mocked. "Hell, *anybody* could write that."

"Yes," said Oscar, "anybody *could*, but Irving *did*."

Fortunately for us all, it is not possible to retire men such as E. B. White.

*When I was young, I pitied the old. Now
old, it is the young I pity.*

Jean Rostand

In his eighty-eighth year, Dr. Gustav Eckstein is even
more energetic and vital than he was at 56, when he
first began to enrich my life.

He continues to write and teach and lecture. Although he has long since passed the mandatory retirement age for professors at the College of Medicine of the University of Cincinnati, he is still there,
still active. Special dispensations have been made for
him, new titles invented, loopholes found. The fact is
that he is indispensable—an institution within an institution, without which it would be dangerously diminished.

So he tears about Cincinnati, making daily visits to
the clinics, as he has done for over sixty years; and
conducts his seminars, the most popular in the history
of the university.

He rises at dawn each morning and goes to work on
whichever of his two books in progress strikes his
fancy. The first is a comprehensive work on Pavlov,
with whom he was once associated. The second, an
autobiography. During the past four years, he has
made three round trips to the Soviet Union, and is

planning another, in order that he may observe, at first hand, a Russian winter. He consults regularly with the Psychiatric Division of the college on a long-range project involving the interrelationship between psychology and physiology. He serves as mentor and invaluable friend to a variety of individuals all over the United States.

He is a perfect example of his own theories on the subject of age and aging, life and death.

I once asked for his views on death.

"Oh, I don't mind the idea at all," he replied. "I'm quite resigned to death, but—but just *not today!*"

Small in stature, he is an immense charged-up dynamo of energy.

He listens even more intently than he talks. His long involvement with the world of birds and animals has made him virtually a vegetarian. He eats little, but claims it is enough.

He avoids medical check-ups, saying, "If anything goes wrong with my body, my body will tell me."

Gustav Eckstein has been kept excitingly alive by constant work, mounting creativity, close and varied interpersonal relationships, never-ending study and learning (at 85, he began to learn Russian to facilitate his work on Pavlov), and by a staggering diversity of interests.

Although he is primarily a physiologist, he can discourse brilliantly and originally on Shakespeare. He is a doctor and a dentist and a scientist and writes marvelous plays. He is a tireless observer of nature, and has written *The Body Has a Head, Canary, Everyday*

Miracle, Lives; a fine novel: *Kettle;* and occasional polemics: *In Peace Japan Breeds War.*

He has written about cockroaches and parrots, and is the author of the most successful medical biography extant: *Noguchi.*

He has traveled to almost every part of the world, has lived and worked in Japan and Russia and France, as well as in the United States.

Again, living proof that it is not activity which wears out the human machine and spirit, but *inactivity.*

"The trouble with mandatory retirement," says Eckstein, "is this: If you tell a man he's going to be retired on his sixty-fifth birthday, it's much the same as telling a man sitting on death row that he's going to be executed on the thirteenth of June. See, these people who know that, who've been told that, I mean the ones who work in businesses, or banks, or universities —they get to be, say, sixty, and what happens? They start to fade a little. And then they get to be sixty-one, and they fade a little more. They're *conditioned,* don't you see—oh, how well Pavlov understood all this!

"They've been told repeatedly that sixty-five equals uselessness. We all know that if you're told something over and over again, no matter how nonsensical it is, you get to believe it. Just the repetition of a myth, hammered into your consciousness, stays there and becomes part of it. Wasn't this the theory that Hitler applied? Well, there you are. If people are made to believe that at sixty-five, they cross the line into decline—well, if there's no resistance to this force, no antidote to the poison, by the time they get to be sixty-five, they're ready—finished. They retire—that is, they *are* retired, and they join the shuffleboard set and fade away. But damn it all, in fact and in truth, some of these people might easily have had twenty or thirty years of important work, of good life, ahead of them. God, if it weren't all so tragic, it would be funny.

"What counts more than anything is the point of view of the individual—the mental superstructural thing. I don't know what this means—I don't *want* to know. In fact, I think life would be less interesting if I did, that God Almighty would be less interesting. If it were clear in my head as the ultimate truth, you see, I'd have it there and I'd be less interested in it. But I'm very interested in it because I never *will* be able to understand it, and I'll be able to go on forever *trying* to understand it. But this far I've gotten as I approach one hundred, this far I have gotten."

"You seem to be placing life in the category of art."

"Am I?"

"Yes—to be saying that living is an art because any art is a striving toward the ideal. If it's ever attained, then it's all over. The energy goes out of it. What matters is the *striving* that produces the art."

"That's right, and what happens is that as people stop striving, they stop living. Or, at least, they begin to waver. The psychological decline begins and the bodily decline follows. Now, I'm not saying that the body couldn't break down any damned time at all, but you've got to remember that in these old creatures there's a problem. If you get the fashion strongly enough inculcated, they themselves begin to teach themselves that they're getting old. I've known men and women, colleagues of mine, scientists who've become isolated and who began to worry and wonder whether they were not *actually* on the way out. And when they begin to think that, they begin to go."

"A kind of self-hypnosis?"

"A young man gets a pain in the belly, he thinks it's a pain in the belly, and that maybe he shouldn't have eaten that second hot dog. An old man gets a pain in the belly, he begins to think, I wonder if I've got cancer of the stomach? And then up in his head where everything has been functioning freely, the thought that maybe he could live forever begins to get muddled, and everything in his head is so much intruded upon by the pain in his belly—of course, it's a physical reality, but it begins to interfere with the reasonable operation of everything in his head. You've got to remember that the aging body is a different thing from the aging mind—about that there isn't any doubt at all. And the aging body does now and then knock at the aging mind. But that proves absolutely nothing about the capacity to ascend at any age."

"*Any* age?"

"Certainly," he said. "There's buried in the nature of everybody exactly what we're talking about. They all know they're going to get old, they're all worried about it, they all think they can push it off—or hope so, anyway, and they all look for things around them to suggest that their survival might just possibly be a little longer than their father had told them it would be . . . look at my own father . . . that's such a strange instance . . . he got to be a dentist in middle life."

"Was he any good?" I asked.

"I'll tell you *how* good. Ten days before he died, I telephoned out to him and said, 'Father, there's a roughness on one of my teeth.'

"He says, 'Well, drive out.'

"So I drive out to this office."

"And how old was he at this point?"

"Nearly ninety-four. Ninety-three and something. He was able to say one afternoon to a teenage patient, 'I looked after your great-grandfather.' So I arrive, and he doesn't waste any time with me. He never did in his life, and he doesn't now, either. He conducts me into his office, I sit down in the chair, he takes up his electric drill, which, remember, is a formidable instrument. I watch his hand. I'm so interested, this quiet hand, it's my head that it's going into, it's my tooth, and I can see that there's not a tremor, there's nothing; he just takes it up quietly and his comment is, 'Your teeth are wearing away a little in front.'

"I say, 'Yes, of course, Father.'

"He says, 'Well, if you don't mind, I don't mind.' And we part on that note.

"It's the last time I see my father, just short of ninety-four, and he's treated me as a patient, with an electric drill inside my head. Well, that's certainly evidence that a man can do almost any physical thing at any age if the orientation is right."

"Can we talk about athletes and athletics?" I asked. "Because so much on the subject of physical ability and deterioration is centered here. What is it that actually happens to an athlete when he gets to be thirty-two, or -three, or -four?"

94

"Well, if you want just an informal opinion, I'd say that he's infested with old age prematurely. I think he *thinks* he's ready to retire. Sometimes they don't fire him right off, but they begin to shrink his salary. In our town last year, they gave Johnny Bench two hundred thousand dollars to catch. He's young, a great personality. But here's Pete Rose, who led the league in hitting; still they trimmed his salary to one seventy-five. Why? Because he's going on thirty-four, and they think maybe he's not such a good risk. Well, all I can say is that Pete Rose won't be quite as good if he ever gets it into his head that he's fading. The truth is there's absolutely no reason why he can't be out there on that field, doing what he's done for several years, keeping the whole team alive. Good God, he kept the whole *city* alive."

"Is there anything in *this*, Gus? Say we do begin to lose physical powers when we get on in years. Isn't there some compensation in the form of experience?"

"Certainly."

"Take Pete Rose—a man who's played three or four thousand ball games. He's seen just about every play there is, and probably won't make as many mistakes as an eighteen-year-old catcher who's got more stamina."

"No question about it."

"And doesn't that sort of thing happen to all of us, even those of us who aren't baseball players?"

"Of course."

"Do you remember a book some years ago about the Supreme Court? It was called *Nine Old Men*, and somehow the title was derogatory. My impression is that the Court is a little younger today than it was, say, thirty years ago. But how far do we want that trend to go?"

"I think it's gotten younger because of the very pelting that we're talking about. Not because of any ulterior physiological reason—it's just been pelted, pelted, pelted, until they *think* they have to push down the age. In Japan, they honor age. But they're a much older civilization. Maybe we'll catch up someday."

From the age of six I had a mania for drawing the form of things. By the time I was fifty I had published an infinity of designs; but all I produced before the age of seventy is not worth taking into account. At seventy-three I learned a little about the real structure of nature, animals, plants, trees, birds, fishes, and insects. In consequence, when I am eighty I shall have made still more progress; at ninety I shall penetrate the mystery of things; at one hundred I shall certainly have reached a marvelous stage; and when I am one hundred and ten everything I do, be it a dot or a line, will be alive. I beg those who live as long as I to see if I do not keep my word.

Hokusai

In South Norwalk, Connecticut, there is a company called Fertl, Inc. The President, Hoyt Catlin, is 87. Most of his exployees are in their sixties. A few are in their seventies. And then there is Emma Wilkins, 83. The average age of Fertl's staff is 71.

Fertl, Inc. manufactures little cubes made of potting soil, moisture retainers, and nutrients; also vegetable or flower seeds. They are used by gardeners as starters.

"Back in 1954," says Catlin, "I had a business installing sound systems in schools. My wife wanted me to find something I could do close to home. Then when we were on a trip to England, I noticed these little cubes in a hardware store. As soon as we got home I made plans to import the cubes here. In 1954 I sold a hundred thousand, all through newspaper ads, and working out of my garage. In 1955 I sold another hundred thousand. Then the English firm stopped making the cubes and I decided to do it myself. That was in 1956. At first I did everything myself. Now I have sixteen people working here. The company's gone from a first year's gross of eighteen thousand dollars to a last year's gross of over six hundred thousand."

Catlin works closely with the Senior Personnel Placement Bureau, a nonprofit organization in Norwalk that helps older people find jobs.

On the subject of retirement, he says, "I was at retirement age when I *started* this business twenty years ago. We've gone from four hours a day, five months a year, to all day, twelve months a year. How could I retire?"

A Connecticut survey found that Fertl, Inc. was one of the most efficient small businesses in the state. It has a virtually zero absentee rate, and practically no employee turnover. The workers at Fertl, Inc. are glad to be there.

One of the employees: "I've met friends of my own

age who retired at age sixty-five and they just go down, down, down, down. There's no interest in keeping young. Oh, sure—I've heard them say over and over again, 'Now when I retire I can get a lot of things done that I have left to do.' So then their wives push them to get those things done. They get them all done, and there's nothing else left. There isn't the obligation to do something every day."

Another was asked, "Why do you go on working?"

"Because it makes me feel so good," he replied. "I think of myself as sixty-nine years young, not sixty-nine years old."

"What do you think you'd be doing if you weren't here?"

"Going crazy, probably. Just wandering around. I mean, I'm a man of a lot of activities, sports-minded and all that, but that's not it, I *need* something—a responsibility."

Most of the employees of Fertl, Inc. are there not because they need the money, but because they desire activity.

To one of its women: "How important is it to be productive at your age?"

"It's everything. If you have something to do, you don't grow old."

And the man working beside her added, "I had fellows in my outfit during the war couldn't wait till they were sixty-two so they could retire. You know where they are today? In the cemetery."

Commissioner Werner H. Kramarsky, of New York's Division of Human Rights, has said that a study of the work performance of state employees 65 and older found them "about equal to and in some instances noticeably better than younger employees in terms of their work performance, attendance records, punctuality, and on-the-job accidents. Thus discrimination against this age group not only conflicts with our goal of equal opportunity, but appears to be contrary to sound business considerations as well."

And Alice Margaret Brophy, of the New York City Commission for the Aging:

"It annoys hell out of me when people say, 'Gee, you look young for your age.' What does that mean? I mean, is there some model in the Smithsonian that you're supposed to look a certain way at sixty-five and seventy-five and eighty-five? You know, you can die old at thirty and live young at eighty. Me, I'm sixty-five and I'm glad I made it. I accept aging as a part of the dignity, experience, and maturity of life. Nothing extraordinary happens to you when you go to bed on the eve of your sixty-fifth birthday. You don't wake up the next day a less adequate person, a less competent person, a less able person. But society regards you as ready for the rocking chair or the ash heap. You're no longer allowed to produce, to work, to make your talents available."

A member of General Douglas MacArthur's staff in Tokyo recalls a sign over his desk which read: "Youth is not a time of life—it is a state of mind. You are as young as your faith, as old as your fear; as young as your hope, as old as your despair."

The younger officers in the General's command used to poke fun at these platitudes. Why? The fact was that there before them in the feisty and powerful person of MacArthur, they saw the result of the application of this touchstone.

Levi Eshkol, the Prime Minister of Israel, died suddenly in 1969. Golda Meir was nominated to replace him. To many Israelis, it seemed a hopelessly misguided appointment. Golda Meir was 71, in semiretirement, often hospitalized, and rumored to be seriously ill. But her nomination seemed the only way to avoid a divisive struggle between Moshe Dayan and Yigal Allon. A poll showed that only 3 per cent of the population approved of her appointment. A few months later, the 3 per cent had become 80 per cent. As for Golda Meir personally—her position, with its difficult duties and wide responsibilities, had apparently revitalized her. She worked fifteen to sixteen hours every day, growing healthier and more vigorous than she had been for twenty years.

What a mistake it is to underestimate or to put down experience. Remember the town that lost its electrical power and blacked out? Efforts to repair the system failed until someone remembered the elderly, retired engineer who had worked on the original installation. He was sent for, arrived, examined the equipment, took a tiny mallet from his pocket, and tapped a switch. The crisis was over. Later, the town clerk received his itemized bill.

SERVICES:	$1,000.02
Tapping:	$ .02
Knowing where to tap:	$1,000.00

> *It pays to stay alive.*
> *Ruth Gordon*

Ruth Gordon is the American actress-writer whose long career peaked in the seventh decade of her life.

I pause, wondering if I should pursue this subject, in view of the fact that she has been, for thirty-five years, my wife.

Gertrude Stein: "Writing is telling what you know."

I proceed because if there is one subject on which I am an expert, it is the subject of Ruth Gordon.

I know how she lives and how she works.

Not long ago, we returned to our home in Edgartown, Massachusetts, following a longer-than-usual absence. On the street we met one of our neighbors and stopped to chat. He wanted to know why we had been away for such a long time. Ruth explained that she had been detained in New York, starring in *The Prince of Central Park*, a film for CBS Television, and that directly following, she had gone to Hollywood to make a feature film for Paramount, and to do two television shows. On her return, she was unable to leave New York since she was involved with Harper & Row in the prepublication activity surrounding her autobiography, *My Side*.

"Well," said our neighbor, "it sounds as though you need to be here for a while now."

"Yes," said Ruth, "but I'm on my way back to California to do a sequel to *Rosemary's Baby*."

"But then back here?"

"No," said Ruth. "We're hardly going to be here at all *this* summer. I've written a play for myself and we're going to do a summer tryout of it."

"Good heavens, Miss Gordon!" said our neighbor. "When do you rest?"

"At night," she answered.

It was not meant as a joke.

Directness and practicality are the hallmarks of her existence.

She feels that part of her strength derives from the fact that she never had an easy time of it. She reminds me that Emerson explained the ruggedness of New Englanders by saying, "From the first, they had to live through those winters and became strong, fighting them."

This explains in part the physical side, and something of the sort is equally true with regard to the rest of her life. At 15, she decided to become an actress: without money, without apparent aptitude, without conventional good looks, without resources.

These debits were outweighed by a single credit: determination.

Today it embarrasses Ruth to be looked upon as a phenomenon. Strangers approach her on the street and inquire as to her "secret." Almost every morning the mail brings similar requests.

There is no secret. What there is, is a desire to work, to create, to stay in action, to be part of the scene.

In the thirty-five years of our marriage, I have never known her to be bored for so much as ten seconds. Thousands of times I have heard her say something like, "This is the greatest apple I've ever tasted." Or: "This is the most remarkable book I've ever read." Or: "Isn't that the most beautiful horse you've ever seen?"

The point being that her appreciation is constantly bringing her new peaks of discovery. Whether this is true or not, she believes it. And that is what matters. She says that nothing is more important than imagination and endurance.

I have seen her, through the years, striving toward discipline and organization. I have observed the remarkable way in which she is able to scuttle the inessentials of daily life, and concentrate on the matter of the moment. She calls it "putting on the blinders."

She is and always has been an early riser. "I like to get up and get out before everybody's used up the good air."

In her sixtieth year, she had one of her greatest theatrical successes in *The Matchmaker* by Thornton Wilder.

It was a play he had written expressly for her seventeen years earlier under the title *The Merchant of Yonkers*, but because of a series of artistic differences as to its production, she did not play it.

In any case, it failed.

Some years later, she and her friend Tyrone Guthrie, discussing plays that deserved a second chance, hit upon this one of Wilder's and agreed to do it—someday.

It turned out that they were the only two who had any desire to revive it, but the more often producers and other players turned it down, the stronger became Ruth's determination to get it on. In time, it happened.

The Matchmaker opened in Newcastle, went to The Edinburgh Festival, the British provinces, The Berlin Festival, London for a year, New York for two seasons, then a glittering transcontinental tour.

At 62, she was the only member of a large company who had played the entire run without missing a single performance.

I recall the Saturday it closed. She had played the matinee at The Huntington Hartford Theatre in Hollywood, and had returned to The Beverly Hills Hotel to rest between performances. When I came in about six o'clock, I was astonished to find her sitting up in bed, her glasses perched on her nose, studying the script! A matter of routine and the discipline of an ordered professional life. This is what she customarily did between matinee and night performances, and the fact that she was about to give her 1,084th—and final—performance in the play did not deter her from her appointed course.

She has not submitted to plastic surgery for the sake of rejuvenation, nor has she achieved her youthful appearance and spirit from pillboxes or elixir bottles.

She still numbers among her friends people who have been in her life since her early youth. She regularly attends her high school reunions (Quincy High

School, class of 1914), and keeps up a correspondence with men and women she has known for sixty and seventy years.

Yet among her closest and most intimate friends these days are the young people she has encountered in the course of her recent work. Natalie Wood, Mia Farrow, Bud Cort, seem to be never off the phone. They are interested in her; she is interested in them and in their problems and careers and aspirations.

Harold and Maude, the film in which she starred with Bud Cort, has proved to be a nonesuch. Relatively unsuccessful at first, this story of a love affair involving an 80-year-old woman and a 20-year-old boy has developed into a cult film. In cities all over the world—especially those with large collegiate populations—it has achieved runs of two to three years. It is constantly revived everywhere. The fan mail is voluminous. Hardly a day passes when Ruth is not approached on the street or in a restaurant by someone who wants to tell her that they have seen the film six times or sixteen times or forty times. In almost every case, it is a young person, although many older people have reported a similar response.

This suggests to me that there is in the psyche of the community a deep, visceral desire for peace between the generations. Although it is the present fashion for the young to express their antipathy toward the old by ridicule or scorn or neglect or enmity or attack, and common for the old to disapprove of the manners and morals and actions and wardrobe and music and language and hairdress of the young, it may well be that these are but superficial manifestations.

Often when the attitudinizing of the day is put aside, young and old live side by side, in close and creative and meaningful empathy.

I, for one, experience it almost daily, cultivating youthful friends and associates. Our beginnings are often sticky with prejudice. But in time, with good will on either side, we find our way to a delightful plateau.

I admire the young people of our time. They are the most alert, educated, informed, sensible generation in history. I believe in their future when I observe how diligently and passionately they address themselves to the things that matter: the air, the water, the earth, nutrition and health, and social order.

One of Ruth Gordon's principles is "Develop built-in confidence."

Also: "Never give up; and never, under any circumstances, no matter what—*never* face the facts."

Her youthful spirit and vitality and, indeed, appearance spring from within. She walks. She thinks. She intends. She hopes. She works. She loves.

*The best way to be young is to hang out
with old people.*

                                        Nipsey Russell

A war is being waged all about us—that of the individual against the forces of overorganization, statistical principles, hard and fast no-exception rules, and
life controlled by thinking machines.

Despite its wonders, the machine—even the thinking machine—is still a machine.

When Dr. Eckstein was writing his towering work,
The Body Has a Head, he asked me if I could arrange
for him to see some of the advanced data computers
in action. I did so, and accompanied him to the sub-
basement of the Time and Life Building where they
were being operated. We spent three and a half impressive hours there. After we left, we walked up-
town. Eckstein seemed to be thinking hard, so I said
nothing for a long time. We walked in silence until
finally he stopped and said, "God!"

"Well, Gus," I said, "I know how you revere the
human body, but at last you've seen something superior to it, haven't you?"

The look on his face told me I had blundered.

"Let me ask you something," he said coolly and

evenly. "If that machine should happen to get damaged, can it repair itself?"

We live too much by statistics and by polls. We attempt to achieve taste and judgment, principle and opinion, not by means of our own cerebration or instinct, but by getting the answer from a machine.

Will the machine, created by man, turn on him and destroy him? To some extent, it has already begun to do so.

A few years ago, Alan Jay Lerner and I agreed that Harry Leon Wilson's remarkable novel *Ruggles of Red Gap* would transfer effectively into the musical theatre.

Investigating the matter, we found that the rights were controlled by one of the major motion picture studios. Together we called on the head of the studio and put our proposal before him.

He responded enthusiastically at once, and had reservations only about the plan of doing it first on Broadway.

"Why not go right into the film version?" he suggested.

We said we would think about it; eventually returned and agreed.

"Fine," he said. "Let me lay it on the boys."

Ten days later he sent for us.

"Bad news," he said.

"What do you mean?"

"Well, it's a funny thing. Everybody here at the studio went for the idea, thought it was terrific right down the line, but then we put it into the computer and the print-out was negative; no, not negative, *very* negative, so that's that."

I could hardly believe what I had heard—that men would respect the "opinion" of a machine more than their own instinct and judgment.

Yet this is happening in thousands of enterprises, and is largely the cause of the shifting standards of retirement and age.

The American Medical Association has never been known as a particularly liberal or progressive organization, yet it has consistently opposed any kind of mandatory retirement age. It has pointed out in lawsuits on every level that it is a dangerous procedure and harmful to the health and well-being of our people.

Similarly, the American Civil Liberties Union, approaching the question from another direction, insists that a person's constitutional rights are being violated when that person is summarily dismissed from work solely because of age. But even with both these powerful forces at work—representing the physical and the philosophical—most of these cases are lost by the victimized individuals.

In the last Presidential campaign, Governor Carter wooed potential voters by asserting that the unemployment rate of 7.8 per cent, or eight million unemployed, was catastrophic, the highest unemployment since the days of the thirties depression.

President Ford countered with the argument that more people were employed in the United States than ever before in our history.

The exchange confused some, puzzled others. Who was right? Both were, of course. Our population is in a permanent state of explosion—more and more people, more and more jobs, food, clothing, shelter, sports, machines, money—more of everything except common sense. There is no question but that an economy of this kind, efficiently organized, can absorb into its labor force every single individual who wants to work, regardless of race or color or sex or age.

One of those who is in favor of systematically replacing the older men in his company is a New York publisher of my acquaintance.

"You've got to get rid of the older ones at some point," he said, "otherwise the younger ones feel there's no opportunity."

"When did you become President of this company?" I inquired.

"Twelve years ago."

"How many people did you employ then?"

"About seventy or eighty."

"And how many do you employ now?"

"About four hundred."

"Well, then, what's your problem?"

"It's a question of economics," he replied. "We can't carry all those senior salaries. Not if we can replace them effectively."

"So it's really a matter of money more than a concern for providing opportunities for the new generation."

"To some degree," he said. "To some small degree."

Intelligent, enlightened organizations use neither yardstick. They have the courage and decency to judge men and women solely on their merits, talents, and abilities. A worker who has become bored or ineffectual should be replaced; one who maintains interest and effectiveness should not be; considerations of age should not enter into the matter at all.

Old age is ready to undertake tasks that youth shirked because they would take too long.

Somerset Maugham

One of America's most fascinating revolutionaries is Miss Maggie Kuhn of Philadelphia. She is part of that parade of American women who have changed the course of our history: Harriet Beecher Stowe, Jane Addams, Lillian Wald, Carrie Nation, Margaret Sanger, Victoria Woodhull. Each of these admirable heroines dealt in a powerful and pragmatic way with an evil of the society of her time.

Maggie Kuhn, at 72, is grappling with one of the most dangerous and virulent diseases of *her* time— ageism. She recognizes that only when minorities organize and demonstrate political power can they hope to find redress from injustice.

To this end, she organized the Gray Panthers.

For many years, she headed the Presbyterian Church Missions, but when she reached the age of 65, even that benign Christian organization retired her.

The proof that this was a cruelly unnecessary act is demonstrated by the fact that now, seven years later, she travels about the country, averaging two lectures a day, three hundred days out of every year; and has grown stronger and more vigorous as a result. The Gray Panthers, which now has over seven thousand members, is composed not solely of graybeards, but has in its membership people from 14 to 90.

Maggie Kuhn herself does not accept the mythic stereotypes of old age: "I don't know why older people believe them, and younger people are taught to accept them—like old people drool; they take laxatives all the time; their sex organs dry up; they can't understand youthful progress and are stuck in the past; this whole idiocy that senility is an inevitable part of age."

The incidence of psychopathology rises with age, as do depression and suicide. The suicide rate, in fact, is highest among white men in their eighties.

Senility, that penultimate stage of life, long thought to be a tragic condition to be accepted, is now understood to be a common but treatable disease. Dr. Carl Eisdorfer, of the University of Washington: "The notion that it's untreatable is nonsense."

When Maggie Kuhn speaks to predominantly female audiences, she urges them to abandon those physicians who refuse to prescribe hormones that ease the difficulties of menopause.

In her active life, she has a drink when she feels like it. She does not smoke, but says that occasionally, when she is around young people, she shares a joint with them. However, she fights against the use of drugs among both young and old, and is especially concerned with the practice of sedating old people into vegetables with tranquilizers. She calls the physicians who practice this method and the pharmaceutical manufacturers "pill pushers," and says, "They have a license to rip off old people and they rip them off every chance they get."

A department of her organization is devoted to ending compulsory retirement. Another branch is working on the subject of liberalized, progressive, and sophisticated sex education.

Maggie Kuhn says, "Some find it hard to believe, but sexual pleasures do not end for older people. This is a myth perpetuated by our adult children who are embarrassed to think that their mothers and daddies have, or had, sex activity. They have an immaculate conception of their own creation. Most children find it difficult, especially when they are in their own middle life, to allow thoughts of their mother and father, or surviving parent, enjoying sex."

She deplores the present methods of dealing with senior citizens in groups that are programmed by younger staff people. "Kindergarten stuff," she calls it, and labels retirement communities "big playpens."

"I am appalled," she says, "at the number of people who have given up but, thank heaven, not all of us are willing to become just wrinkled babies."

The personality of a society is often reflected in its humor. Not so long ago, stuttering comedians could count on easy laughs; drunk acts were in vogue; and a retarded person or one with a harelip was considered fair game for humor. We seem to have progressed beyond such barbarous ideas. How long before the elderly cease to be the butt of too many contemporary jokes?

The Gray Panthers recently added a project called Media Watch to their program. Lydia Bragger, who heads this committee, says, "We are against television stereotypes that show older people as helpless and decrepit."

A special target will be "The Carol Burnett Show." Maggie Kuhn says, "It's disgusting. On nearly every show, a character comes on stage drooling, senile, and slack-jawed. Some older people do lose control of their mouth muscles; it's irreversible and it's not funny. On the show, this female character is brought out for a good laugh, and what's worse, everybody laughs."

Lydia Bragger adds, "She demeans older people with ridiculous dialogue about sex, implying all they can do is put their false teeth in the water at night. The idea that they are so limited makes older people look useless and helpless."

It is easy to take offense, to feel hurt and humiliated, and to bitch about it. It is harder, but better, to take action. That is the strength of the Gray Panthers movement. They have arranged meetings with CBS executives and plan to present protests to the National Association of Broadcasters Television Code Board, which regulates network programs.

It is astonishing to observe how frequently *The New Yorker*, that most sophisticated, literary, and intelligent of publications, falls into the trap of raising cheap laughs at the expense of the aged or the aging. Hardly an issue is without one or more cartoons exploiting the comic possibilities of older people. Here is the sort of thing *The New Yorker* has run during the past year:

> A middle-aged couple is sitting at a coffee table. The choleric husband says:
> "Quit telling me you're only as old as you feel. I feel like I'm a hundred and forty."

> A scene in a men's club. Two old crocks are observing a third. One of them:
> "Old Whittington figures if he makes it through March, he's good for the rest of the year."

> A fat and ugly-because-old couple sit at a dinner table with wine glasses raised. The man is saying: "To your continued survival!"

> A startled woman on a tropical lawn sees a tiny creature in oversized clothing dashing out of the brush crying: "Wifey! Wifey! I've found the Fountain of Youth!"

> A group portrait of miserable men and women. Over their heads a banner reads: "WELCOME TO THE PEACEFUL ACRES HOME FOR THE MIDDLE-AGED."

People who are bombarded with jokes and anecdotes and witticisms of this sort across the years can be easily conditioned into impotence or diminished sexual activity simply because they are led to believe that it is the natural order of things.

The research and experience of the growing school of sex therapists do not support these myths. Men and women can and do experience sexual difficulties even in their twenties and thirties, and there are many sexually active men and women in their seventies and eighties.

The dreaded male climacteric and the female menopause have been proven to be physiological phenomena unrelated to sexual action. Indeed, there are many cases of women whose indifferent sex lives have *improved* in later life.

But myths die slowly, and the earlier an erroneous idea is implanted, the longer it takes to excise it.

*Today I have completed 64 Springtimes
and I am now in much better health, much
stronger, much more active, than I ever
was in my youth. . . . It is quite wrong to
think of old age as a downward slope. One
climbs higher and higher with the advanc-
ing years, with surprising strides.*

George Sand

Not long ago, Marian Hart flew her 14-year-old sin-
gle-engine Beechcraft plane from Washington, D.C.,
to Gander, Newfoundland; to Reykjavik, Iceland; to
Dublin, Ireland.

She is said to be the oldest woman ever to fly the
Atlantic alone. Maybe. Marian Hart was only 83.

No sensible citizen denies that the institution of
Medicare is valuable, needed, utterly civilized.

The error lies in the arbitrary age—65—established
for eligibility. The United States Government has,
however inadvertently, given respectability to the in-
anity of setting a specific age for aging.

I have many friends in their seventies, and at least
three in their eighties, who have never taken advan-

tage of their Medicare benefits. Several have not even signed up for the service.

Conversely, friends in their forties and fifties who would be greatly benefited by Medicare have to wait for help until they reach the magic number.

There has been some agitation of late in Washington about *lowering* the age of Medicare. A few Congressmen have recognized Medicare as a valuable re-election issue. The opposition is to the cost, but pressure mounts along with the danger that the label of obsolescence will soon be put on people of 62, then 60, 55, 50. The direction is unmistakably downward.

If present trends continue, one out of every six men from 55 to 64 will no longer be in the work force by the time he reaches 64. Ten years ago, the figure was only one out of every eight.

The American educational system began to make sense from the time it realized that all students do not learn at the same pace. A brilliant student of mathematics, who grasps the subject swiftly and easily, might find it difficult to parse a simple declarative sentence. Some students have mechanical aptitude, others do not. A few are interested in poetry, most abhor it. And these interests or apathies surface quickly in some young people, slowly in others.

Thornton Wilder had one pupil at Lawrenceville, when he was a master there, who appeared to be constantly preoccupied and looking out the window. It was impossible to gain his attention on *any* subject. The faculty agreed that the boy was probably retarded. He was put through endless psychiatric tests, disciplined, expelled, reinstated, and finally, simply shoved through and out. Wilder reported that years later, he encountered the dim-witted chap. In adulthood, the fellow had become one of the most distinguished ornithologists in the world. In his youth, he *had* been looking out the window—at birds, the only subject in which he had a real interest.

Our strength lies in our differences, in our diversity of interests and talents.

We age differently, and even the causes can be diverse: physical, mental, emotional, occupational, or geographical.

No matter how many numbers are attached to us, we should take care never to forget our names.

We find statistics dull until we understand that we are part of them. For instance, older persons in the United States—those 60 and over—today constitute our largest and swiftest-growing minority. Women of 35 today have nine out of ten chances of reaching 60; a man, eight out of ten.

The number of older Americans is over 31 million— a sizable force which could be politically effective if organized.

The 21 million persons on Social Security alone represent more than the population of twenty states and more than the total labor union membership of the entire country.

More significant is the fact that while the population of the United States is three times what it was in 1900, the number of older people is *eight* times as large.

Political analysts are agreed that in the last national election, the black vote, and especially the Southern black vote, was responsible for Jimmy Carter's victory. A maligned and maltreated minority, organized and educated, became a decisive political force.

Similarly, the power of the over-60 minority needs only to be marshaled to restore justice and order.

Sophisticated legislators know something more: that this group is potentially the most powerful minority in the land because it has, by far, the highest voting percentage of any bloc. Whereas in the 1976 election only 52 per cent of all eligible voters exercised their franchise, and only 28 per cent of those under 30 did so—*78 per cent of our older citizens voted.*

The condition of the mature, and by that one must mean everyone over 40, is poor but by no means hopeless.

There are at present over three hundred organizations that concern themselves with the problems of aging. Among them: the Gray Panthers, the American Association of Retired Persons, The Sixty-Five Club, the Retired Professional Action Group, The Forty-Plus Club, the National Caucus for Older Americans, the National Alliance of Senior Citizens (headed by Curt Clinkscales III, 30 years old!), the Asociación Nacional Por Personas Mayores, the Urban Elderly Coalition, the Forum for Professionals and Executives, the American Geriatrics Society, Community Concern for Senior Citizens, the Senior Citizen Internship Program, the National Caucus on the Black Aged, the Gerontological Society, the American Aging Association, the Oliver Wendell Holmes Association, the National Association of State Units on Aging, the Institute for Retired Professionals, the National Association of Retired Federal Employees, the Institute of Lifetime Learning, the National Retired Teachers Association, the Division of Adult Development and Aging of the American Psychological Association, the International Federation on Aging, the National Center on Black Aged, the International Senior Citizens Association, Inc., the National Council of Senior Citizens, and the National Council on the Aging.

Offshoots and splinter groups and spin-offs proliferate. One of the most active groups dealing with the problem is the National Council on the Aging, headed by Mother Bernadette de Lourdes of the Carmelite Order. Action is the key term. Political pressure is a pragmatic tool. The exposure of the senselessness of the present fashion by means of ridicule and humor is additionally valuable.

Maggie Kuhn: "Our throw-away society, with its matching throw-away mentality, scrap-piles people as it does old automobiles. Little help has been given to relieve the terrible anxieties and frustrations of age. Such understanding and corresponding efforts of our own to give longevity some meaning and purpose are needed. Otherwise, life-extending measures are but more evidence of ageism—cruel experimentation with elderly guinea pigs. We act on the discovery of gerontologists that the harder we work, the more likely we are to stay well and alive. Total rest is almost a sure way to bring on physical and mental degeneration. We believe sexual interest and activity are needed in

125

the lifestyle of older adults. They provide the basis for self-esteem and an energizing force that invigorates body and mind."

Suppose you are 40 or 50 and unhappy in your job. In all probability, you are trapped, since the job market is narrowing for people in their forties and closing for those in their fifties.

Forced retirement creates and perpetuates the myth that old age is not a productive period, and encourages the idea that people should spend their later years in nothing more than recreation.

In the larger sense, forced retirement removes needed skills and experience from the labor force and isolates older people from other groups, thus depriving society as a whole of their energy and experience.

A most encouraging development is the growing practice of retired men and women undertaking consultantships in the fields of their expertise. This plan benefits both the consultant, who stays in action and alive, and the employer, who gains the inestimable contribution of wisdom and experience.

In 1967, Congress passed the Age Discrimination in Employment Act. A step in the right direction, but a stumbling step—because it provided protection for those between 40 and 65, no protection whatever for those beyond 65.

Our civilization is treating its older people in the way that we are told certain primitive, barbarous, uncivilized tribes treat theirs. They throw them away. When a member of a tribe becomes old, he or she is taken to a high cliff and ceremoniously pitched into the rocky valley below.

Anthropologist Colin Turnbull, who lived for three years with the Iks, the nomadic Ugandan tribe, learned that they systematically destroyed both the very old and the very young in their number. For them, this ritual represents a desperate economic matter of survival—of life and death, a necessity—but can we say the same?

Our own method appears, on the face of it, to be more humane, but is it?

In the play *Tobacco Road*, the old grandmother chews her turnip on the periphery of the family, virtually ignored by them. One day she is missing. When Jeeter Lester is informed of this, he says, "Oh, yeah. We oughta go out and look for 'er—one of these days."

Millions of us who saw the play laughed at this line without thinking that to some degree many repeat the pattern in their own lives. We have all known persons in reasonably good health and spirits who went to a retirement home or community as a matter of economic, or geographical, or family convenience. Have we not observed the acceleration of deterioration in these persons? Few ever leave those places alive . . . and knowing it makes them less likely to live.

*It is abundantly apparent that we are not
only wasting the talents of our unemployed
adults and the potential of our young, but
neglecting the continuing contribution of
our elderly as well. And, in doing so, we are
not only losing the people's faith in society's institutions, we are wasting the very
life of this nation.*

Hubert Humphrey

The strength of any country is based on its ability to
marshal effectively its manpower and woman power.

To do this, it is imperative that use be made of all
able-bodied citizens without regard to sex, or color—
or *age*. But at present, of the 1.1 million older women
in the labor force, more than half are interested in
full-time jobs and cannot get them.

The American South is gaining strength and power
and importance because it is learning, by means of racial integration, to make full use of all its people.
When older people are denied a place in the scheme
of things, many of them, through no fault of their
own, become a burden to society, and are thus segre-
gated.

As the young have had no experience in dealing

with youth, so the old have had none in dealing with age. Each period of one's life is a foray into a strange new land.

The science of gerontology is comparatively new and, like other sciences, it has within it conflicting schools of thought. Out of disagreement and challenge, experiment and proof, continuously developing wisdom comes to the fore.

On one finding, however, all gerontologists agree: that a human being must remain active at the peril of stagnating; that the elixir of life is mental activity and acquisition; that maturing men and women must avoid ruts, fixed habits, old ways; that the antidote to aging is action, both physical and mental, and learning. It scarcely matters what form the learning takes —a language, a manual skill, riding a bicycle, preparing a soufflé, bookbinding, dressmaking, mastering a musical instrument—so long as the process of taking in is kept alive.

The importance of adult education cannot be stressed too strongly. Up to now in the United States, such education has been regarded as a harmless pastime akin to bingo, shuffleboard, and needlepoint— something to occupy the time of people who have nothing better to do, a means of keeping middlescent delinquents off the streets. Is this so?

By and large, adults make superior students because they understand and appreciate the meaning and importance of education.

Many young people go to school because they are forced to do so by their parents, by law, by convention.

Even on the high school level, the major thrust appears to be getting by the regents. And our colleges are filled with great numbers who scrounge for a degree of one sort or another with one eye—the principal one—on the football field or the basketball court. Surely this cynical attitude toward education results in the sort of cheating scandal recently revealed at West Point, which spotlights the false relationship of students to the very *idea* of education, to preparation for the future. For *who* is cheated if one is there to learn?

On campuses in the United States, there is a lively and flourishing business in the marketing of exam papers, term papers, and doctoral dissertations. A bright young relative of mine worked his way through college writing and selling masters' theses.

I have yet to hear of a single case of cheating or fraud in any area of adult education. Grownups who undertake a course of study do so because of the desire to learn. No one who has spent a few years out in the great world can fail to have an appreciation of the importance of knowledge, skill, information, and culture.

An enlightened society understands that education should be a continuing, never-ending process.

Some progress in providing broad opportunities for such activity in the United States has been made, but much more is needed and at an accelerated speed. In each of the Scandinavian countries, programs of adult education abound, and the record shows that many unknown, unsuccessful persons have achieved late success and even greatness as a result.

Denmark, for over a hundred years, has had a system of "folk high schools." Today it has eighty of these, an impressive figure for a country of just over five million citizens. These schools teach literature, social studies, foreign affairs, psychology, music, and foreign languages, especially English. Most Scandinavians speak English. How many Americans command a second language?

Sweden has a comparable system, with an extended curriculum that includes mathematics, hygiene, drama, music, art, and in addition, "domestic arts," offered now to both sexes. Its expressed goal is "to improve the student's power of independent thinking and critical judgment and further his maturity and his interest in learning." According to this goal, every folk high school determines its own approach.

Norway and Finland also have such programs, which, because of the countries' economic structures, reach more firmly into the unions and the working classes.

Half of the adult population of the Scandinavian countries takes part in continuing education. Would this not be a better use of our senior citizens' time than the hypnosis induced by indiscriminate television watching, sports, or simply sitting still?

All these countries, in addition to offering cultural programs, have more pragmatic forms of education: vocational training and retraining; job-betterment courses; the development of skills according to aptitudes.

It has been argued that the Scandinavian system is not applicable to the United States because the median age of Americans is 25, as compared to 48 for Swedes.

Still, educational opportunity should be made available to that part of our population which wants it and needs it.

There are signs that the United States is beginning to catch up. At the Fromm Institute for Lifelong Learning of the University of San Francisco, seventy-three people, all over the age of 50, were enrolled. Courses in philosophy, psychology, history, economics, English, science, and anthropology were conducted by retired university professors.

At the neighboring San Francisco State University, any citizen over 60 may sit in on any course free of charge so long as the instructor gives permission.

A study conducted at Puget Sound Health Cooperative in Seattle demonstrated that a person's abilities *do not* necessarily decrease with passing time. In fact, verbal-comprehension skills frequently *increase* with age.

There is no reason why an older person cannot acquire new knowledge and new skills.

On the subject of senility, it has been learned that deteriorating mental conditions are sometimes the result of too much self-medication. Very often, if the person is put under a physician's care and withdrawn from the drugs, the so-called senility disappears.

Another cause of apparent senility may well be poor nutrition. When a person's income is cut, which often happens to older people, the first things to be cut back are food and transportation. The result is elderly people who are inadequately nourished and isolated from the rest of society.

These views are tragically supported by an official survey made by the Community Service Society and the New York City Department of Social Services, which revealed that 8 per cent of the elderly poor in the Supplemental Security Income Program considered themselves "worse off" than they had been a year earlier. Eight per cent of them said they could not afford to eat a single balanced meal a day, 18 per cent said that they had difficulty in managing food purchases.

This, in the most powerful, affluent, and productive country in the world!

Dr. Richard L. Sprott, a psychologist working in behavioral studies at the Jackson Laboratory in Bar Harbor, Maine, recently announced that his experimental evidence suggests that it is time to reassess the view that learning depends on age.

"Aging itself is not detrimental to learning ability and I.Q.," he said. "The key factor instead is the health of the individual as he grows older."

He concludes that the ability to learn and I.Q. do *not* decrease with age but, in fact, remain steady and, in some cases, even increase, depending upon the individual, his profession, interests, and, most important, health.

In the Utopian sense, it is easy to imagine a design of life according to this plan: childhood and learning; adolescence and education; the years of youth, during which the education is applied; the middle years of work and achievement; finally, the later years filled with leisure or teaching or travel or a second career or, most important of all, a return to education.

In 1962, an enterprising and imaginative man named Hy Hirsch founded the Institute for Retired Professionals (IRP). It has become part of the New School for Social Research in New York City. Its one thousand members take part in a unique educational program in which they both teach and study.

Among the participants are retired doctors, dentists, business executives, bankers, artists, journalists, teachers, lawyers, and engineers—all teaching, all learning.

Shades of Plato on West Twelfth Street.

Hirsch believes that the mind is the one part of us that does not stop growing, but that programs for the aged tend to be paternalistic, geared to the lowest common denominator. For all his ebullience and enthusiasm, he is an unassuming man, but in the strictest sense, a lifesaver. One has only to spend a few hours in the company of this remarkable group to realize that the unused mind and the fading spirit are every bit as tragic as the dying body.

New ideas, new subjects, new faces, prove to be more effective than new wonder drugs or new vitamins. At present, the IRP offers some sixty-six courses, including: Our Changing Culture; French, Italian, and Hebrew; workshops in writing and poetry; dramatics, music; various history courses; and studies in biomedical developments. Each course is coordinated by one of the members, who decides how the course is to be conducted: preparation of papers, theses and dissertations, discussions, performances, field trips.

Each member pays $200 a year, and is permitted to take as many courses as he wishes. The Institute is entirely self-supporting and makes no claim upon either the city's or the state's educational resources.

The strength and importance of this idea are reflected in the way branches of the Institute are proliferating. New York already has a number of offshoots and there are similar institutes in Boston, Philadelphia, Cleveland, San Francisco, and San Diego.

There are people, more and more of them every day, who are saying "No" to oblivion.

> *The man who is too old to learn was prob-*
> *ably always too old to learn.*
>
> > *Henry S. Haskins*

On June 25, 1976—four years after Robert D. Murgia began his suit—the Supreme Court of the United States handed down one of its dippiest decisions. By a vote of seven to one, Mr. Justice Stevens abstaining, and Mr. Justice Marshall dissenting, it ruled that the State of Massachusetts was *not* in violation of the Constitution when it summarily discharged Murgia from its police force for no reason other than that he had reached his fiftieth birthday.

The decision *against* him contains the following passage:

> . . . and there is no dispute that, when he retired, his excellent physical and mental health still rendered him capable of performing the duties of a uniformed officer.

Despite that admission, the spectacle of a Court with a median age of 64 ruling that a man of 50 is obsolete has overtones of the off-with-his-head court of *Alice in Wonderland*. Without, alas, its charm.

Surely physical and mental examinations should have been the overriding considerations, and not the whimsical given number. Is it not entirely possible that under the Massachusetts procedure a less qualified, albeit younger, man might be replacing Murgia?

The Supreme Court, having ruled, now becomes defensive:

> The class subject to the compulsory retirement feature of the Massachusetts Statute consists of uniformed state police officers over the age of 50. It cannot be said to be discriminatory only against the elderly.

(How's that again?)

> Rather, it draws the line at a certain age in middle life.

(Oh.)

> But even old age does not define a "discrete and insular group," *United States* v. *Carolene Products Co.*, 304 U.S. 144, 152–153, n.4 (1938), in need of "extraordinary protection from the majoritarian political process." Instead, it marks a stage that each of us will reach if we live out our normal span. Even if the statute could be said to impose a penalty upon a class defined as the aged, it would not impose a distinction sufficiently akin to those classifications that we have found suspect to call for strict judicial scrutiny.

(Translation, *please!*)

Toward the end of its lengthy decision and self-defense, the Court begins to feel unsure of itself, and one can almost see its frown on the printed page:

> But where rationality is the test, a State "does not violate the Equal Protection Clause merely because the classifications made by its laws are imperfect." *Dandridge* v. *Williams,* 397 U.S. at 485.

Finally, waffling pathetically, and having condemned Murgia to superfluity along with who knows how many others:

> We do not make light of the substantial economic and psychological effects premature and compulsory retirement can have on an individual; nor do we denigrate the ability of elderly citizens to continue to contribute to society. The problems of retirement have been well documented and are beyond serious dispute.

Except for Mr. Justice Marshall's blazing dissent, it was over, then, for Lt. Col. Robert D. Murgia.

Anthony Trollope about his mother:

. . . In 1844, she moved herself to Florence, where she remained till her death in 1863. She continued writing up to 1856, when she was seventy-six years old,—and had at that time produced 114 volumes of which the first was not written until she was fifty. Her career offers great encouragement to those who have not begun early in life, but are still ambitious to do something before they depart hence.

Dear Mrs. Trollope. Born in 1780 with a severely limited life expectancy, she nevertheless lived a hard life, reared a large and illustrious family, nursed her invalid and maladroit husband as well as several of her children through lingering illnesses, and produced a river of books. Moreover, she lived to be 83. How lucky she was not a state trooper.

It was not the climate of Florence that extended her span of life, but rather the ceaseless activity and occupation, which generated boundless energy and surging life force.

A century later, George Burns, busy at 80, said, "I can't die. How can I die? I'm *booked!*"

At present, the question of our older citizens must be considered a minority problem, and we have been less than effective in dealing with our minority problems across the years.

Baseball clubs appear to deal with the matter of retirement far better than banks or universities. When a player, due to the passage of time, can no longer compete effectively, he is frequently shifted to the coaching staff. Still others become scouts seeking out fresh talent and a few move into management or administration or sportscasting. The point is that they are not all, because of age, relegated to oblivion.

One must be concerned with the problems of age when one is young.

An Edgartown neighbor of mine, George-Henry Medeiros, told me once that his Portuguese mother had taught him the most important lesson of economy. "The time to economize on your sack of potatoes," she said, "is when it's full. If you wait till you get to the bottom of the sack, it's too *late* to economize."

When one's sack of years is full, one should give some thought to passing time and the future.

At the University of Maryland's Center on Aging, funded by a grant from the American Association of Retired Persons, a year-long study of children's attitudes toward the elderly was made. One hundred youngsters from 3 to 11 were interviewed.

In general, the kids had a negative view of the elderly, thought them "sick, sad, tired, dirty and ugly," and decided never to be old themselves. A few of them thought the elderly "friendly, good and kind," but even so, objected to them because they were "wrinkled, crippled, chew funny, and haven't got any teeth."

As the researchers went more deeply into the study, they found that the very young usually have limited contact with the elderly and almost no knowledge whatever of what it means to be old.

Is it not important that the young be oriented to the whole idea of aging, its strengths as well as its weaknesses?

Education can demonstrate that age is an element of life to be anticipated, *not* feared; embraced, *not* repulsed.

"What we're trying to do is dispel a little bit of ignorance about what it means to be growing old," says Edward Ansello, Associate Director of the study.

The situation is undeniably serious, the problem vexing. Is there a solution? If there is, the cause will first need to be isolated. What *is* the cause? There is wide and violent disagreement on this point. The battle rages.

Some blame the present economy, which is based upon the commercialization of the young. Such a system has no use for the elderly.

Others insist that tension between old and young has always been, is now, and always will be—and that any attempt to change this is doomed to failure since it deals with the basic meanness of human nature.

Still others see it as an artificial situation created by the advertising business.

Increasingly, children brought up in a climate of disrespect for their elders begin to see only their bad points and resent all older people as being unpleasant.

It is unfair to the *young* to condemn them to a warped view of older people; it limits their opportunities for fruitful friendship; it diminishes their chances for acquiring wisdom, perspective, patience; it narrows rather than enriches their circle of acquaintance; it denies them delight (he who has seen a young person who is friends with an older one has seen a kind of beauty); and it denies them life. For they will fear age from the time they are 20—worried about 30, frightened of 40, fearful of 50, scared of 60, silly about 70.

*Enthusiasm in maturity—that's the great
trick of life.*

Dr. Fred Plum

Your outlook, your frame of mind, as you advance in years is what matters most.

Sigmund Freud's mother was extraordinarily pretty, knew it, never forgot it. Her son gave her a shawl as a ninetieth-birthday gift. She returned it, saying, "It makes me look *too old!*"

When she was 95, a picture of her appeared in a Viennese newspaper. It was shown to her. She slapped it away in a temper, shouting, "That's not me! That's somebody who's a hundred!"

For her production of *The Cherry Orchard*, Margaret Webster engaged A. G. Andrews for the role of Firs, the old caretaker.

Pogey Andrews was 87, at the time the oldest working actor in America. On opening night, Miss Webster went backstage to the dressing rooms to wish her cast well.

When she reached Pogey's room, she found him sitting in front of his makeup mirror, carefully painting wrinkles onto his forehead!

There are various avenues open to those who refuse to be relegated to the dump heap of life.

One is continuing education. Present-day colleges number among their students many men and women who have retired; an increasing number of women, having completed their mothering roles, have picked up again on an interrupted or neglected education.

One of the students of LaGuardia Community College in 1975 was Mrs. Elizabeth Sarcka. Two years earlier she had been in an automobile accident and was told to resign herself to the fact that she would never walk again. She proved the doctors wrong and at 81 moved about the streets of New York and the campus at LaGuardia at the same pace as her teenage fellow students.

Mrs. Ester Domash, a sophomore at Bronx Community College, studying philosophy, English and Jewish literature, asked: "Does school belong only to the young? Because a girl reaches eighty-one doesn't mean she stops thinking, feeling, hoping. Water that doesn't move stagnates. Running water is always fresh."

Another road to a long life is that of a second career. This may involve the development of a hobby or subject of interest into an occupation; or teaching; or becoming a consultant; or going into business for oneself—alone or with partners who find themselves in a like situation. Still another is entry into social service on either a paid or volunteer basis.

There are many others, limited only by the imagination and enterprise of the person who understands the dangers of retirement—such as William Tierney of New York City.

Mr. Tierney has spent his working lifetime serving the City of New York, mainly as Deputy Assistant Corporation Counsel attached to the office of the Mayor. He is a highly respected, greatly loved, essentially happy man.

Five years ago he reached the compulsory retirement age of 65, and was given an extension because no one in his department could imagine it functioning without him.

A year later, a second extension; then another. After this, it was doubtful that more could be arranged, so on October 1, 1975, William Tierney was retired.

"The next day, October second," he said, "I just came in and continued to do my job. I don't know if anybody knows I'm retired. Maybe they'll throw me out when they find out."

Not likely. Bill Tierney created a personal approach to the plaguing problem. Although he was in one of the city's highest salary brackets at 68, giving up the money did not matter to him. What *was* important was his job, so he forfeited salary and substituted his Social Security and pension. The idea of being removed from his post, after forty-eight years, was unthinkable. He continued to turn up daily to do his job. He did not feel he was doing anything altruistic or holier-than-thou.

He had served in every administration from Joseph V. McKee to Abraham D. Beame.

Bill Tierney, in his own way, beat the system. When it was suggested to him that to have taken this course of action he must love his job, he looked startled. "No, I don't *love* it. It's satisfying." And when asked how long he planned to go on, he replied, "As long as I can keep going."

In the 1976 elections, S. I. Hayakawa, 70, won the Republican Senatorial nomination in California, running against a strong field which included Robert Finch, 50, who had been Lieutenant Governor of California and, later, Secretary of Health, Education, and Welfare under President Nixon.

Hayakawa had scant political background. A noted semanticist, he had spent his life in the academic world. Moreover, he had been a registered Democrat until three years before he ran for office as a Republican.

During the campaign, the question of his age arose.

Hayakawa's response: "Before World War II in Japan they killed off all the older politicians. All that were left were the damn fools who attacked Pearl Harbor. I think that this country needs older statesmen too."

Apparently, the voters of California agreed with his sentiment because when the election itself was held, Hayakawa easily won the Senate seat over the incumbent, Senator John Tunney, 42.

His victory is the more impressive considering that registered Democrats outnumber registered Republicans in the State of California by a margin of three to one.

Here is a vital, active man, beginning a completely new career at the age of 70, ten or eight or five years *after* most employed men are expected to retire, or are forced to do so.

The fact that Senators are elected for a six-year term did not appear to trouble the voters. They realized that Hayakawa would still be serving them in the Senate at the age of 76.

At 73, Dr. Benjamin Spock, the renowned pediatrician, brought his forty-eight-year-old marriage to an end. He faced the fact too few are willing to face: namely, that his marriage had worn out.

He has changed his lifestyle, works only on alternate months, and spends every other month sailing in the Virgin Islands. He has remarried, since he has a strong belief in the institution.

Dr. Howard Rusk, at 76, is head of New York University's Institute of Rehabilitation Medicine, as well as the World Rehabilitation Fund.

His hair is thinning, but has not turned gray.

"I can still work a twelve-hour day without too much of a problem," he says. NYU has wisely suspended its mandatory retirement rule for Dr. Rusk. He intends to go on working indefinitely.

"I've got awfully good genes," he says. "I can never really retire. I can hardly wait to get to work every morning."

In Yugoslavia, Marshal Tito, 85, is the powerful and effective head of state.

The remarkable R. Buckminster Fuller, also in his eighties, continues to exercise his soaring imagination and to produce new inventions to put beside his geodesic dome and Dymaxion dwelling machine.

And at 83, George Meany remains the vigorous, militant head of the AFL-CIO and its fourteen million members.

When Bishop Robert B. Gooden of Los Angeles reached the age of 100, he offered his resignation to his diocese. It was refused on the grounds that he was still alert, capable, irreplaceable.

Peter Grimm, founder of the Citizens Budget Commission, one of New York City's most valuable entities, is active in its operation. He goes to work daily at William A. White & Sons, the real estate firm. Mr. Grimm is 92.

On another level of human occupation, we find Samuel Rosenthal, who turns up six days a week at the H. A. Eisner window shade company in Manhattan. He cuts, sews, and tacks window shades, and has been employed by the Eisner firm for eighty-four years. He is 96, and started work there when he was 12.

"It's a steady job," he says.

When the Prime Minister of Great Britain, Harold Wilson, resigned, he was quoted as saying, "Well, I'm sixty, don't you know, and I'm too old for this job."

He was immediately replaced by Leonard James Callaghan, who was 64, but who obviously did *not* consider himself too old for the job. What does this prove? Age is a state of mind—or mindlessness.

Walter Hoving runs Tiffany & Company, and is one of the most innovative and daring merchants in New York. "I think this mandatory retirement business is for the birds," he says. "Mr. Tiffany ran this place until he was ninety-two, and I'm only eighty."

In 1976, the New York Stock Exchange found its operations confused and inefficient. William M. Batten, retired from the J. C. Penney Company, was called in to become Chairman of the Exchange. Mr. Batten was 67.

Similarly, William M. Blackie, 72, was recalled from retirement to resume the leadership of the troubled Genesco Corporation.

More and more, older and experienced executives are finding themselves in demand.

In his monumental work, *Age and Achievement*, H. C. Lehman concludes that the notion of man's creative accomplishments occurring mainly in early or middle life is *absolutely fallacious*. His long research, as well as his painstaking statistical studies, reveal a staggering body of work in education, mathematics, natural history, medicine, the arts, and politics accomplished in maturity:

● Giovanni Bellini, at 86, was acknowledged to be the best painter in Venice.

● Cervantes completed, at 68, what many believe to be the greatest novel of all time, *Don Quixote*.

151

● Charles Dana, at 74, wrote the classic *History of Medicine*.

● Duméril, the French zoologist, finished his definitive work on reptiles at 80.

● Galileo did his most important work in his seventies. His lasting contributions in the field of astronomy were made in his very late life, and he continued to work until the day of his death.

Dr. Lehman made an in-depth study of the life and work of Thomas Alva Edison. He found that Edison's peak was reached at the age of 35, but that he experienced a second at the age of 57 and a third between the ages of 70 and 75. Edison remained active and productive until 83.

Georgia O'Keefe is still painting daily at the age of 90. Her latest work is considered her best by experts, and in her ninetieth year, she added literary expression to her graphic work, publishing her first book.

Specious observers who claim that creativity begins to diminish in middle life should be reminded that Richard Jordan Gatling, inventor of the Gatling gun, turned his attention to agricultural implements and at the age of 82 invented the motor-driven plow.

Thomas Hardy's truly great period was his last, and his finest poetry was written between the ages of 75 and 85.

Clara Barton, founder of the Red Cross, working fourteen hours a day at 90: "While the strength is given me, I have no right to lay it down."

Victor Hugo celebrated his eightieth birthday by completing one of his greatest works, *The Legend of the Centuries,* an account of history through the ages based upon Biblical lore, mythology, and folk tales. At the banquet of homage, he said, "Gentlemen, I am eighty and I am beginning my career!"

Samuel Johnson's contributions to the English language and literature are widely known. His most celebrated work, *The Lives of the English Poets,* was completed when he was 72.

At 73, John Parkinson wrote his book on botany which is still standard.

At 76, Herbert Spencer wrote the last volume of his *System of Synthetic Philosophy,* and continued to revise the complete body of his work year after year, until he was 80.

In the early nineteenth century, when Col. John Stevens was 76, he built a circular railroad track on his lawn in Hoboken, New Jersey. An account reads: "He then built a locomotive which ran on the track before the amazed throng. He was not content until many of them had ridden on it. This was the first operation of a steam railroad in America."

Alfred Lord Tennyson was still producing poetry in his eighties. Giuseppe Verdi capped his career at 80 with *Falstaff.* At 85, he was still composing.

In the summer of 1975, Justice A. David Benjamin of the Brooklyn Appellate Division of the New York Supreme Court, reached the age of 76 and was retired. He had figured he would cross that bridge when he came to it, so he promptly crossed the bridge to Manhattan and joined an active law firm as a senior partner.

Jacob Stillman was a unique figure in the history of

the New York City public school system. His pupils, year after year, refused to permit him to retire. By special dispensation, he went on teaching into his nineties. On his ninetieth birthday, *The New York Times* asked him to what he attributed his great age. He replied: "Well, in all my years, I never wasted any energy resisting temptation."

It is frequently argued that all these examples are meaningless since they were or are of *outstanding* older people and therefore cannot be considered models of what *anyone* can accomplish.

The rebuttal is that we have no way of knowing whether these people accomplish because they are unusual or unusual because they accomplish. In most cases it may be that productivity and longevity go hand in hand.

It has been my observation that the average man is unusual, if indeed there is any such being as the average man or the average woman. A woman of 72 in Colorado was tested by the Department of Motor Vehicles and was found to have the same reactions as did young Air Force Academy cadets. Charles Atlas, the professional physical culturist, was doing two hundred push-ups daily at the age of 75. How many 20-year-olds can do *twenty* push-ups? Thomas Bridson, on his ninety-ninth birthday, successfully climbed a two-thousand-foot mountain. There are farmers in their nineties at work everywhere in the world.

One of the best-known anecdotes in show business concerns the partnership of George M. Cohan and

Sam H. Harris. An aging, talented, and temperamental actor in one of their productions had behaved reprehensibly, then quit, without giving notice.

"Let's never hire the son-of-a-bitch again," said Cohan, "until we need him!"

The same sort of benign hypocrisy is practiced quietly by organizations who change the rules when it suits them. The practitioners of this cop-out include the United States Navy. The Navy's strictly enforced mandatory retirement age is 62; but Admiral Hyman G. Rickover, 77, is still on duty as the head of the Navy's Nuclear Propulsion Program, and was recently reappointed to two more years of active duty. The Navy keeps "hiring" him. Why? Because the Navy needs him.

*People who don't cherish their elderly
have forgotten whence they came and
whither they go.*

Ramsey Clark

Mrs. Lou Glasse, Director of the New York State
Office for the Aging, says, "Too many people are embarrassed about the aging. They are a source of great
skills and manpower that we have not made enough
of in our country."

Dr. Patrick J. Montana, President of the National
Center for Career Life Planning, predicts that in
about twenty-five years, forced retirement at 55 will
become the norm, at which time there will be 57 million people over 55, compared to 40 million today.
This will be caused primarily by the influx of young
people moving into the job market during the next
few years.

Dr. Montana observes that the pressure for early retirement is so great that it has created dangerous
stress among older workers.

Many sociologists urge the adoption of educational
programs to help men and women to cope with retirement living, which can stretch out to a quarter of a
century or more, as life expectancy grows.

One says, "The vast majority don't know *how* to retire. It's a profession, like any other. You have to approach it rationally. If you don't have the necessary ingredients, you can't build a contented retired life."

A retiree who tried living in a retirement community left it after a short time, saying, "Hell, I don't want to hang around all the time with people my own age. Just because I'm a fuddy-duddy doesn't mean I want to live with other fuddy-duddies."

Forced early retirement, says Dr. Montana, ranks *ninth* among the forty top stress producers in our nation, coming directly after death of a spouse; divorce; marital separation; a jail term; death of a close family member; personal injury or illness; marriage; and being fired.

In 1935, the Social Security system was instituted in the United States. Each working citizen became a number as well as a name. The concept of Social Security is not only correct, but vitally important to progress. In realistic terms, however, it stands as a failure because the system has lost touch with reality.

Security. That was the word. The individual and the government working together were going to provide security for the individual at the proper time. But the fact is that after thirty or forty years of consecutive labor, the *maximum* benefit to which a worker is entitled is about $425 per month. Security? As it exists today, Social Security is no more than guaranteed annual poverty.

The system has within it other small tumors, such as the rule that limits allowed earnings. If more is earned, the Social Security check is reduced. This encourages *inactivity* by mandating penalties for *activity!*

One has only to read the original Social Security Act, full of progressive ideals and noble purpose, and compare it with its daily application in contemporary life to see how obsolete it has become.

Reform must begin with government itself on the federal, state, and civic levels.

If the *government* takes the lead in getting rid of its workers at an arbitrary age, is not the private sector encouraged to follow suit?

In 1977, thousands of New York City employees were "separated" from their jobs because of age by the Beame administration. Not "fired," an official explains—merely "separated." The New York City Employees Retirement System claims that it has no precise figures.

In 1977, Mayor Abraham D. Beame was 71 years old.

Ewan Clague, who once served as Commissioner of the United States Bureau of Labor Statistics: "We are *loading* the retirement system with enormous burdens. To encourage retirement at age fifty-five, for example, this nation has got to be crazy."

On the federal level, the Manpower Administration of the Department of Labor in 1972 published a booklet entitled *Back to Work after Retirement*. In it, the following reasonable passage appeared:

> You want to be useful. In many jobs the very qualities that go with age are bonuses. . . . You have experience, skill and stability, and

159

the good judgment that goes with a long
time of work. You are conscientious, loyal,
hard-working, because you want to make
good. Our Nation cannot afford to waste
valuable manpower. There are too many
jobs that need doing.

But lost in the maze of Washington bureaucracy,
half a million left hands have not the foggiest idea
what half a million right hands are doing, and frequently even the *right* hands do not know what *they*
are doing. In the same booklet, which stated categor-
ically that "the Federal Government evaluates each
applicant for a job on ability and age . . . there is no
maximum age for federal jobs," it also said:

> Persons under seventy can qualify for regu-
> lar appointments, while persons over seventy
> can receive only temporary appointments
> subject to renewal.

This in a city that has seen distinguished, history-
making Justices on the Supreme Court bench in their
eighties and nineties; which has profited by the wisdom and experience of Senators and Congressmen in
their seventies and eighties; which has had experts in
every branch of government who were invaluable
and indispensable precisely *because of* their age and
experience.

Recent legislation promises to abolish *any* retirement age for federal employees. In the past, they were
constantly being pressured into early retirement, offered bonuses and fuzzy incentives and mixed-up

arithmetic. In 1972, the Nixon Administration attempted to get a bill through Congress which would have given the President power to set maximum age limits for the five hundred job classifications in the federal work force. It was roundly defeated in the House of Representatives. Representative Herman Badillo of New York argued forcefully against it: "Present medical examinations for entry into the federal service are ample safeguards to determine conclusively whether an applicant can properly perform on a job."

On the municipal level, matters are frequently just as misguided. New York City, suffering a financial crisis, was forced to consider every sort of economy measure.

One bonehead idea was to get highly paid civil servants to leave their jobs before the then mandatory retirement age of 65.

Extensions past that age, which had always been common, would be refused except in the "most critical cases."

Why is it that no one reminded Mayor Beame what happened when this system was attempted in 1968, involving Transit Authority employees? An agreement between the TA and the city include a "sweetener," giving the employees retirement benefits based on the wages they had earned in their final year of employment. Naturally, the veteran employees built up overtime to swell their pensions. The scheme proved to be disastrous because the mass exodus of experienced workers created a vacuum that took years to correct.

The military establishments are the worst of all, having the power to retire soldiers and sailors, whether enlisted men or officers, after twenty years of service, regardless of their age or experience or abilities.

The problem is not indigenous to the United States. It is international, and dealt with as clumsily in France, England, Italy, Japan, and the Soviet Union as it has been in our own country.

In 1969 the United Nations organized a study of retirement encompassing every member nation and in 1972 published a report saying:

> The long-range overall picture is of a world with an aging population. This poses a new challenge—with social and economic considerations not yet understood.

It advises that the "over sixty-fives" are proliferating, and continues:

> Most countries won't be able to afford—culturally, psychologically, and financially, to go on supporting such large dependent populations without serious social changes.

The report proposes that the standard retirement age should be *raised* rather than *lowered*.

Sweden, that model of social enlightenment, now discourages retirement and has raised its retirement age to 67, but this is still unsatisfactory to those who believe *no* age should be set; that each person should be considered individually.

Dr. Robert N. Butler, one of the outstanding experts in the field: "There is irony in the way older people are welcomed back into the work force when a nation needs them, as Japan, the U.S.S.R. and others are doing today and as the United States did in World War II." The old did their part in achieving the victory. Winning the peace will be an even greater triumph.

Philip Dunne has said, "There are some things worse than war and better than peace."

For decades, the sick situation was with us on a continuing, day-to-day basis. Each day of the year, over four thousand Americans reached the age of 65, entering what was called "statutory senility." They were legally declared to be superannuated, obsolete, useless. Legally, because even in such legislation as existed, the age-discrimination laws protected only those between 40 and 65.

All this was a result of one of the best-intentioned yet ill-advised acts ever undertaken by the United States Government. Before the Social Security Act, the Federal Government had no provision for retirement at any age, nor did most businesses.

But then a committee began to draft a bill establishing some sort of social security and the number 65 came up. Why? How? Professor Douglas Brown of Princeton was on that committee and says, "I can remember no suggestion of another age."

Were statisticians and sociologists consulted or was it, as some believe, an automatic, unthinking echo of Bismarck's foul idea? In any event, it was a convenient number. At the time the Act was being discussed, 25 per cent of the labor force was unemployed and knocking off those over 65 was attractive because it improved the statistics.

Moreover, the original idea of social security was meant to apply only to workers who worked with their hands. Many categories were excluded. Teachers did not become eligible until 1950, and for other professions, it was even later.

The bill, when ready, was literally rushed through the House and the Senate. None of the members of either body could have given much thought to the profound effect this new law would have.

Some employers have favored mandatory retirement because it gives them economic advantages—replacing older employees with younger, less experienced ones —and because it removes the nuisance of testing. Also, a uniform retirement age makes it simpler to work out complex retirement and fringe benefits.

The new legislation will permit private industry to enforce mandatory retirement at 70. Progress. Up to now, the law has offered *no* protection on this matter. Bit by bit, we become civilized.

Certainly one should retire if one wishes to. The argument here is against *forced* retirement.

A poll by Lou Harris revealed some unsurprising figures. Younger people thought the mandatory retirement age should be *lower* than 65, but of the citizens over 65 who were asked to respond to the statement: "Nobody should be forced to retire because of age if he wants to continue working and still is able to do a good job"—86 per cent responded *affirmatively!*

Another Harris Poll showed that 40 per cent of the twenty million or more Americans who are now on Social Security would prefer to work.

There is a whale of a difference between a ditch-digger and a lawyer when it comes to retirement. A ditchdigger may be physically worn out by 65 or 70—or just tired of shoveling earth. A lawyer, because of his years of practice, may well be at the peak of his usefulness. It is idiotic to attempt to set a number—any number—that will apply to all people at all times. And even if 65 *did* make sense in 1935—which it did not—even 70 is no longer accurate since it does not take into account the increased life span.

Dr. K. Warner Schaie of the University of Southern California: "The data about stability of intellectual performance certainly argue for a re-examination of mandatory retirement policies. Age is a totally inappropriate criterion for determining whether or not performance is adequate for a given vocational skill. . . . If we had to select a chronologically meaningful retirement age today, it would have to be at least a decade later than would have made sense twenty years ago."

One of the most reasonable retirement proposals is the idea of *gradual* retirement, a phased-out work program; workers deciding at some given point to work shorter hours, to take longer vacations, thus allowing both the employer and the employee to adjust to eventual retirement.

This plan is being tested in various parts of the country with great success.

To characterize American business as the villain in this drama is too simplistic. Thousands upon thousands of employers and leading executives *oppose* mandatory retirement. A survey conducted by the publication *Nation's Business,* asking the question: "Should retirement be mandatory at a certain age?" brought a *negative* response from *four out of five* readers.

The President of Modern Plastics, Inc., of Hialeah, Florida, A. H. Metz: "Many men and women are old at fifty, while others are still active and can contribute their share and more at seventy. Why put those others out to pasture?"

The Vice President and General Manager of Roberts Paper Company, Amarillo, Texas, Frank Stewart: "We have some sales people who were retired at sixty-five and still are very productive ten to fifteen years *after* retirement."

Paul Sperling, Vice President of Corrick International of California, Inc., Santa Cruz, takes an even stronger position: "I believe forced retirement is illegal. If we may not discriminate in *hiring* on the basis of age, then we may not so discriminate in *firing*. The argument that jobs are created for younger workers is specious; the older ones will be leaving the work force soon enough."

From Boston, James J. McCormick, an Assistant Vice President of Liberty Mutual Insurance Company: "Forced retirement because of age is more discriminatory than discrimination because of sex, color or creed; it strikes everyone. It is also *morally* wrong because it denies older citizens their basic civil rights. It deprives them of dignity, a sense of being needed or wanted."

And F. P. Kinsley, Jr., President of Kinsley & Sons, Inc., St. Louis: "I have seen many business associates who were required to retire at sixty-five or seventy. They were extremely active, loved to work, and were a real asset to the company. The adjustment to retirement was often very difficult, and many of them died within a year."

A Midwestern executive: "If judges, politicians, and members of Congress are not forcibly retired, why should anyone else be?"

Many thought forced retirement because of age unwise since it placed too heavy a burden on Social Security, and frequently caused serious financial problems in the retirement programs of many companies.

A number of the most progressive and enlightened company heads supported the aforementioned idea of gradual or phased-out retirement.

The survey revealed that some employers actually *preferred* their older employees, pointing out their superiority in experience, wisdom, loyalty, and dependability.

Not by physical force, not by bodily swift-
ness and agility, are great things accom-
plished, but by deliberation, authority, and
judgment; qualities with which old age is
abundantly provided.

Cicero

In 1950, the Hastings College of Law, in Stanford, adopted a rule against hiring anyone *under* the age of 65 for a full-time professorship. Hastings insisted that a man who is qualified, able, experienced, and fit to continue with the same work in which he was engaged at 64 should not be deprived of the right to do so because he has had another birthday. Dean David E. Snodgrass: "One man is too old to do effective work at fifty-five or sixty. Another is still approaching his peak of efficiency."

He submitted that Benjamin Franklin was 70 in 1776 when he sailed to France in an attempt to enlist its aid in the American Revolution. At 75, he negotiated the peace. At 81, he saved the Constitutional Convention. Dean Snodgrass reminded us that on November 30, 1939, Winston Churchill celebrated his sixty-fifth birthday, and he wondered what the consequences for history might have been had Churchill been forced to retire on that date.

Hastings' remarkable institution, known throughout the academic world as The Sixty-Five Club, came into being as a matter of emergency.

Dean William M. Simmons died suddenly in the summer of 1940 at the age of 55. The academic year 1940–41 was less than five weeks off. A substitute had to be found. The only source of experienced educators appeared to be the compulsorily unemployed. Emeritus Dean Orrin K. McMurray, 70, was recruited. He had taught at Hastings from 1902 to 1904. And Professor Arthur M. Cathcart returned to teach two years after he had been dropped from the Stanford Law faculty.

Suddenly, the country was involved in World War II. Young teachers were scarce. Dean McMurray was replaced by Edward Thurston, 67, for whom there had been no room at Harvard Law School when he attained the age of statutory senility in 1942.

On V-E Day in 1945, the Hastings student body numbered 37. By August 1946, it was 483. Professors were needed, but young men with teaching experience were impossible to find. So Hastings offered jobs to other victims of retirement: Oliver L. McCaskill, 68, of the University of Illinois; and Chester G. Vernier, 65, of Stanford. A year later, with the student body still burgeoning, Hastings added Professor Augustin Derby, 65, of New York University; and soon afterward, Ernest G. Lorenzen, 70, of Yale; Dudley O. McGovney, 71, and Max Ravin, 68, of the University of California; Everett Fraser, 70, of the University of Minnesota; and George C. Bogert, 65, of the University of Chicago.

Before long it became known in academic circles that Hastings was the place where competent law professors over 65 were welcome. The faculty and the student body grew. By 1960, the average age of the faculty was 72 plus. Professors in their late fifties and early sixties were turned away as being underage.

The system was made possible because when the school was founded in 1878 by Serranus Clinton Hastings, the first Chief Justice of the California Supreme Court, with an endowment of $100,000, there was nothing said in the foundation act about retirement. Thus the Board of Directors is free to employ teachers of law at any age and to keep them as long as their services are needed.

Roscoe Pound, Dean Emeritus of the Harvard Law School and the grand old man of American legal education, taught there and wrote that he regarded the law faculty of Hastings as the strongest in the country.

A report states: "The students have discovered that their professors are not only uniquely dedicated teachers, but that they are also more tolerant and understanding than most younger men would be. . . . The members of The Sixty-Five Club are alert, brisk, vigorous and salty-tongued and they are clearly getting a whale of a kick out of life. For they are doing what they like best."

Who has not heard of Colonel Sanders' Kentucky Fried Chicken? Many have wondered if Colonel Sanders is a real person, or merely the creation of a promotional brain. He is real.

Colonel Harlan Sanders was retired at the age of

65. His first Social Security check was for $105. An amateur cook, whose specialty was Kentucky fried chicken, he used part of that $105 to market and promote his recipe. Eight years later, at the age of 73, he sold the franchise rights to his recipe and logo for $4,000,000, plus an arrangement to act as a paid consultant and promoter.

By and large, every successful enterprise is the result of one individual's imagination, enterprise, and perseverance.

Benjamin Duggar, an able professor of science, was forced out of his position when he reached retirement age. He applied to the Lederle Laboratories for work. Fortunately, this is one of the companies without an age prejudice.

At the age of 73, Professor Duggar developed and perfected the remarkable and invaluable antibiotic drug Aureomycin, which is credited with saving hundreds of thousands of lives.

The older people in any society have valuable and vital contributions to make to it, and it is a blunder to dismiss them from our society.

Life is not, or should not be, a spectator sport. It must be lived, not observed.

We are so preoccupied with our search for commercial energy that we lose sight of the fact that we are failing to make use of our full potential of *human* energy. There it lies, bottled up by indifference and neglect and cruelty and ignorance. It sits on park benches, in the game rooms of retirement homes. It is playing bingo and backgammon; wandering aimlessly about the country or the world, taking pictures of itself.

We must, at our peril, begin to find ways to harness this indescribably massive natural resource.

We vie daily for superiority over the Soviet Union. We race to the moon, to Mars, to beat them there. We plunge to the bottom of the sea when we hear that they are doing so.

If we can marshal the full strength of our population by creating opportunities, not only for the old, but for the young as well, other considerations will pale.

A young philosopher: "In the most enlightened and progressive civilization, the elderly are considered to be the most valuable and important members. They are able to warn the succeeding generations of the mistakes they themselves made so that the mistakes will be rectified rather than repeated. The healthy and wise among them provide not only example but inspiration."

At 65, James Michener reflected that in Japan at that age, one received a red kimono and became an elder whose advice was sought.

He was asked to imagine what his life would be like if he were indeed Japanese.

"I would have less money," he replied. "I would have a position as an elder statesman, a more substantial voice in public morality, in public opinion.

"In other societies, at the extreme, a great ceramicist or a great actor is a national treasure. But ours is not a society that honors age."

The laws of our land are meant to be used; to be enforced by the government; to be enjoyed as a protection by its citizens.

While it is true that litigation is a lengthy and often costly process, whenever and wherever possible men and women should take advantage of statutes and ordinances; and, above all, that apex of man's sense of order and right—the Constitution of the United States. The decision in a lawsuit may not always be just, but this should not deter us from pursuing the redress of grievances by way of the courts.

In Detroit, Michigan, the widow of a former executive of the Ford Motor Company sued the company for $1,500,000, based upon the claim that the company's pressure on her husband to take early retirement drove him to suicide.

Technically, Mrs. Helen Sexauer charged age discrimination and breach of contract.

For thirty years, William Sexauer was employed by the Ford Motor Company, working his way up to Manager of Operations in the Accounting Department of the Tractor Division. Then, in an effort to force him to retire, the company began lowering his job-performance rating.

It was changed from "Excellent" to "Satisfactory Plus," a rather tenuous distinction. Yet Sexauer understood the meaning of this gambit, and on May 28, 1973, he retired himself definitely, finally, and dramatically, by killing himself.

Are suits of this kind precursors of others to come? Can companies be forced to include retirement age in contracts? Is it not possible that prospective employees will favor companies which do *not* have such clauses in their contracts?

Since American business is based upon competition, might not the absence of a forced-retirement clause be a great inducement at the time when companies are vying with one another for available young talent —offering free homes, cars, and golf club memberships? What if one progressive company offered the future? How swiftly the others would copy!

In 1977, a bill was passed in the New York State Assembly that would prohibit government agencies and private employers from forcing workers to retire at the age of 65. It was sponsored by Assemblyman Thomas R. Fortune of Brooklyn, and would supersede the present state laws that set mandatory retirement ages for judges and for State Policemen.

"Our bill would not prevent people who wish to retire from doing so," said Fortune, "but by doing this now, we can help the elderly continue their careers if they want to contribute more to pension funds, and draw out a similar amount of such funds after they do retire."

Supporting it, Assembly Speaker Stanley Steingut said, "The bill represents a radical departure from past practices and attitudes concerning the elderly. The generally accepted view that a person should retire at sixty-five is arbitrary. Further, it is intolerable in human terms, and unaffordable in economic terms."

Mostly, it is the elderly who preserve a human link with the past and nourish an entire generation curious to know its full cultural heritage.

Hedrick Smith

Since I am, and have been for a lifetime, theatre-oriented, I tend to view matters in terms of drama.

A well-known theatre precept states that almost anyone can write a first act, but that it takes a playwright to write a second act, and a genius to create a third. I see lives about me conforming to this precept.

"Life," said Ben Franklin, "like a dramatic piece, should not only be conducted with regularity, but methinks it should finish handsomely."

Certainly the first part of most people's existence is comparatively simple. We are more or less cared for; our wants and needs are provided; our duties and responsibilities are minimal.

The second part becomes more complex. We deal with competition, frustration, dashed hopes; we come to grips with compromise and with reality. Still, the struggle is interesting, and whether winning or losing, we are at least in the game.

Now comes that dreaded third act. Consider how

few among us achieve a good one. Good last acts are as rare in life as they are in the theatre.

I once had occasion to discuss this analogy with Laurence Olivier. He was then in his middle fifties—a dangerous age for an actor—and appeared to have exhausted the possibilities of his talent, even though it is the greatest acting talent of the century. He had played every important leading Shakespearean role, an imposing range of contemporary plays and classics, had directed and produced films and plays, had known movie stardom. There seemed to be no worlds left to conquer. Olivier was not only fatigued, but tired, and there were, from time to time, small but significant signs that his career might indeed be fading. He talked of this possibility lightly, certainly without bitterness, then after a few more drinks, said, "I'm going to have a smashing third act!"

We laughed.

In the next fifteen years, Laurence Olivier made his most impressive contributions to the theatre. He gave memorable performances—in *King Lear, The Dance of Death, The Entertainer, Becket, Othello*. He directed superbly, became head of Great Britain's National Theatre, and led it to glory. While acting and producing and administering this superlative theatrical organization, he planned and supervised the construction of the new National Theatre, and became Lord Olivier, the first theatrical figure to be made a peer of the realm. Yes, a *smashing* third act.

Nobody got to be old nowdays.
Manuel Rosario

In the significant, historic case of Robert D. Murgia, it remained for Mr. Justice Thurgood Marshall, dissenting, to keep the Court in touch with reality. Apparently he was unable to persuade a single *one* of his brethren to join him in common sense.

He wrote:

> There is simply no reason why a statute that tells able-bodied police officers, ready and willing to work, that they no longer have the right to earn a living in their chosen profession merely because they are 50 years old, should be judged by the same minimal standards of rationality that we use to test economic legislation that discriminates against business interests. . . . Yet, the Court today not only invokes the minimal level of scrutiny, it wrongly adheres to it.

Then, since precedent is the cornerstone of Supreme Court decisions, he asked them to record that the Court had earlier ruled:

> In so far as a man is deprived of the right to labor his liberty is restricted, his capacity to

179

earn wages and acquire property is lessened, and he is denied the protection which the law affords those who are permitted to work. Liberty means more than freedom from servitude, and the constitutional guarantee is an assurance that the citizen shall be protected in the right to use his powers of mind and body in any lawful calling.

It is possible that Mr. Justice Marshall's feeling for the elderly is a result of his compassion for *any* member of a minority group. He is the only Justice of the Court who has had the experience of living as part of a social minority.

It is to be hoped that others will not be deterred from pressing similar claims because of this misguided adverse decision. It stands on spindly legs and can be upset on the same sort of technicality as that on which it was based.

There is *no* mandatory retirement age for Justices of the Supreme Court of the United States. The American Medical Association and the American Civil Liberties Union noted this fact in the *amicus* briefs which they filed in support of Colonel Murgia.

Ironically, Murgia's wife, Margaret, is employed by the Internal Revenue Service. Under the new law, she will not be forced to retire.

Since Murgia is and always has been an active man, retirement came hard. New employment was complicated by the fact that he made no secret of the fact that should he win his suit—and he had every hope of doing so—he planned to return to the State Police force. This stated resolve kept him out of work for three years, during which his wife supported him and their two sons. Murgia received no financial assistance with the considerable legal fees. He and his family fought out the case as a matter of passionate principle. To relieve the tension of this difficult period, he took up a new hobby. He bought himself a saddle horse named Gentleman Jim, and learned not only to ride but to jump. Those who see him daily at The Andover Riding Academy, galloping Gentleman Jim and taking daring jumps, can hardly believe that this unwrinkled, dark-haired daredevil has been retired from the police force because of age.

Conversely, in Long Beach, California, Robert N. Haughton, 77, is still serving efficiently and effectively on the police force. He is protected because there was no provision for mandatory retirement when he joined the force in 1920.

Justice Marshall said it all at the conclusion of his blistering dissent:

> While depriving any government employee of his job is a significant deprivation, it is particularly burdensome when the person deprived is an older citizen. Once terminated, the elderly cannot readily find alternative employment. The lack of work is not only economically damaging, but emotionally and physically draining. Deprived of his status in the community and of the op-

portunity for meaningful activity, fearful of becoming dependent on others for his support, and lonely in his new-found isolation, the involuntarily retired person is susceptible to physical and emotional ailments as a direct consequence of his enforced idleness. Ample clinical evidence supports the conclusion that mandatory retirement poses a direct threat to the health and life expectancy of the retired person, and these consequences of termination for age are not disputed by appellant. Thus, an older person deprived of his job by the government loses not only his right to earn a living, but, too often, his health as well, in sad contradiction of Browning's promise, "The best is yet to be/The last of life for which the first was made." . . .

I see no reason at all for automatically terminating those officers who reach the age of fifty; indeed, that action seems the height of irrationality.

Ernest Hemingway felt strongly that the worst death for anyone was the loss of what formed the center of his life and made him what he really was. "Retirement," he said, "is the most loathsome word in the English language."

We sometimes hear the argument that if older, entrenched members of a company are not systematically displaced, the younger, upcoming ones will suffer.

Wrong. Every organization attempts to recruit, employ, and promote able newcomers. "There's always room at the top!" Who wants advancement merely because the person ahead has been pushed out for committing a birthday? And would not any intelligent, foresighted young person prefer to join a company with *no* mandatory retirement policy?

In our society, women do not castrate men so much as younger men castrate older men. The aging man worries more about the loss of his job than he does about the loss of his virility.

In the law of the jungle, enforced by claw and fang, the leaders of packs of beasts survive only until the younger grow strong and fierce enough to eliminate them. Do we not follow this same law in a somewhat refined way?

There are hopeful signs. In Seattle, Mayor Wes Uhlman recently abolished mandatory retirement throughout the city's municipal work force to eliminate "arbitrary discrimination against older Americans." He added that the previous system had "robbed the city of a much valued resource—the experience and talents of senior citizens."

In Los Angeles, voters have overwhelmingly passed a similar amendment.

Happily, the private sector has traditionally followed the lead of government in employment practices.

We are waking up.

Straw in the wind? Gerber Products, specializing for years in baby foods ("Babies are our business, our *only* business"), has now diversified, shrewdly, into selling insurance designed principally for the mature. ("Gerber now babies the over-50s.")

A discussion of the subject by two passionate partisans:

"All right. Agreed. It makes its point. Forced retirement and the way we treat our elderly and all the rest of it are unjust. Unwise. Criminal, even. But what about a company's problems?"

"Problems, sure. But not unsolvable. Anyway, having used up the best years of a guy's life—shouldn't a company give him a say about the rest of them?"

"Yes, but what if he becomes senile or disabled? Or erratic or incompetent?"

"Get rid of him, of course. If there's a reason. But not just because of age."

"And pension plans. What about *them*? How's a company supposed to handle all that without a regular system?"

"Easily. Unless their bookkeeper happens to be Uriah Heep. Also—here's a chance for the bloody data computer to atone for some of the damage it's caused us. Listen, when forced retirement is prohibited by law—you'll see—everybody'll all of a sudden figure out how to handle the consequences."

I listen with interest, trying to see both sides.

In the end, I reflect that the times may indeed be out of joint and, as O'Casey's Captain Boyle put it:

'. . . th' whole worl's . . . in a terr . . . ible state o'chassis!"

Still, I persist in my belief that a nation which successfully put men on the moon can also put men on earth.

> Youth is a gift of nature; age is a work of art.
>
> Anon.